FATAI KASALI

Explore a Path to Godly Decision-Making

'Decision Making' copyright © 2018 Fatai Kasali.

The author has asserted his right to be identified as the author of this work in accordance with the Copyright, Designs and Patents Act 1988.

All rights reserved. No part of this publication may be reproduced, stored in a retrieval system, or transmitted, in any form or by any means, electronic, mechanical, photocopying, recording or otherwise without the prior permission of the author.

All Scripture quotations, unless otherwise indicated, are taken from the Holy Bible, King James Version, Cambridge University Press, Oxford University Press, Harper Collins and the Queen's Printers.

Published in the United Kingdom by Glory Publishing

ISBN: 978-1-9996849-0-7

ACKNOWLEDGEMENTS

To God be the glory for the grace to write this book. I give God all the praise and adoration for giving me the inspiration through His Spirit. This has made possible the writing of this book.

My wife, Felicia Ebunlomo, gave me priceless support during the writing of this book. My two sons, Daniel and David, have been very supportive.

To all those who have contributed one way or another to the beauty of this work, thank you very much. May God Almighty bless you all.

INTRODUCTION

Life is about decision-making. We make a series of decisions every day.

Deuteronomy 30:19: "I call heaven and earth to record this day against you, that I have set before you life and death, blessing and cursing: therefore choose life, that both thou and thy seed may live…"

In this Bible verse, God presented two options to Israel. They had to make a choice. He advised them to choose life instead of death. Despite God's advice, Israel retained the freedom to choose. Unfortunately, some Israelites chose the option of death and they died in the wilderness. Those who chose death did not do it intentionally, but their decision to ignore God's advice led them into the consequences of their option. There is a price to pay for every bad decision, and a reward for every good one. It is therefore imperative that you make the right decisions, especially in dangerous circumstances where the price tag on your decision is very great and irreversible.

In life, you will always have right to exercise your free will when it comes to decision-making, so this can affect you for good or ill. It is therefore vital that you learn how to make good decisions, and that depends on the level of knowledge and wisdom you possess.

This book has been written to help you make wise decisions as you face many incidents on the journey of life, and to understand some of the signs of right decisions. The book explores various reasons why your decision-making could be wrong, and the biblical approach to such situations.

It is vital to note that risk is always an issue when it comes to decision-making because every decision carries a certain level of uncertainty. This book will help you deal with the risk aspect of decision-making. You will know how to identify good and bad risks.

Don't forget the wisdom to aid decision-making that is given in this book. It is impossible for you to exercise wisdom that you lack, so absorb it from this book. It will expose you to the various ways to increase your wisdom, and this will prove invaluable to your success in decision-making.

It is my prayer that this book will empower you and greatly aid your decision-making. May God bless you as you read this book.

CONTENTS

1	Guidance for decision-making	9
2	Guidance from His voice	17
3	The red flags!	33
4	Evidence of wrong decisions	43
5	Decisions in diversities	49
6	Why people make wrong decisions	65
7	Dealing with your wrong decisions	135
8	Risk	141
9	Wisdom for decision-making	151

One

GUIDANCE FOR DECISION-MAKING

A decision is the act of making up one's mind about a certain situation. It is usually reached after consideration of various options, opinions, facts and figures. Our whole life is about decision-making. We make a series of decisions almost every minute or hour of the day. Different decisions have diverse implications and price tags. It is therefore very important that you get your decisions right. There are some decisions you can make by yourself, but for others you will need to rely on the help of different people who have better experience.

Using the Bible in Decision-making

2 Timothy 3:16: *"All scripture is given by inspiration of God, and is profitable for doctrine, for reproof, for correction, for instruction in righteousness…"*

The Bible is the Word of God given to man to show us the right decisions in life.

It should be clear that when we say the Bible is the Word of God, it does not imply that every word in the Bible is spoken by God, but that God has given us the Bible as His approved manual for guidance and knowledge. The whole book is inspired by Him, but not all the words in it are spoken by Himself. There are words in the Bible spoken by the devil, demons, angels, men and even animals. God in His wisdom has incorporated a lot of characters in the Bible, whose words and stories give us understanding about those characters and what they can teach us.

For example, Satan is mentioned in various places in the Bible. It gives us a picture of how he speaks, manipulates, steals, destroys and kills. The Bible also reveals to us; the limitations of Satan. It teaches us that Satan can be defeated by man under the cover of the blood of Jesus.

We also see in the Bible how Satan influenced the decision-making of many people and led them into disobedience. In many situations in the Bible, Satan spoke words to mimic God so as to deceive those that listen to him. It is therefore very important for you not to ignore the possibility of deception from Satan during your decision-making. He is able to speak lies into the mind of man. He can speak into one person's mind to deceive another. But your constant study of the Bible will reveal to you; the secrets of Satan's schemes and tricks.

The Bible also shows us different human characters acting in varied situations so that we can learn from their lives. The stories of these Bible characters reveal their strengths and weaknesses. These were incorporated in the Bible so that we can avoid their mistakes and copy their strengths and so live a more Christ-like life. You will read in the Bible how the people of the past responded to different pressures and trials. You will also read in how people obeyed and disobeyed God in their decision-making when they experienced temptation, suffering, blessings and all the circumstances of life.

The Bible also reveals to us how God related with His people in the Bible. God's instructions to Israel in various specific situations educate us in what is permissible and not permissible by God. And finally, the Bible expresses the mind of God about various issues of life by means of His prophets, apostles and teachers in the Bible. These are all intended to guide us in decision-making.

Nevertheless, it is important to state that the Bible does not expressly touch on certain issues that we may face and need to decide upon. There are some specific issues that the Bible does not declare either wrong or right. In some situations, such issues are expected to be dealt with according to the culture and tradition of the people, the general principles given in the Bible and the leading of the Holy Spirit today.

For example, the Bible does not equivocally declare whether some foods or drink are wrong or right to consume. Nor does it go into detail about what our reading habits should be, what entertainment we should watch today, what kind of clothes we should wear for certain situations, etc. Decisions that involve such issues are expected to be taken based on prayer and guidance from the Holy Spirit and His quiet witness in our hearts, and the New Testament makes it clear that on some issues what is right for some Christians may not always be right for others.

While the Bible does not clearly condemn eating of certain foods, you can be specifically instructed by the Holy Spirit not to eat certain foods at a certain time or place or for a particular reason. That may be for your own health or conscience, or it may be in order not to lead others into temptation who may have a weakness for some foods or drink. Such guidance is specifically for you and not for everybody you will come into contact with. Do not make a personal revelation become a general revelation for everyone else.

That said, the Bible contains a wealth of specific guidance on a whole range of subjects that are of major importance to humanity in every time and place. For example, there is more than enough information in the Bible about marriage, business, relationships, etc. When you need to make a decision that concerns any such issue, it is your responsibility to search through the Bible and find the guidance

God has already given. You don't need guidance from anybody else when you are dealing with issues that are clearly stated in the Bible. What you need to do is just obey.

For example, you don't need any guidance on whether to lie or not. It is clearly written in the Bible that you should not lie. This is one of many biblical principles that are not subject to human opinions or interpretation. (There are circumstances in which it is more loving to keep a secret and not disclose the truth about something, as our ultimate principle is always love, but that is not the same as lying.)

The Process of Decision making

1. Clarification of the issue

The first thing you will need to do when making a decision is to identify the issue under consideration. For example, it could be who to marry or the kind of job offers to accept.

2. Biblical exploration

You will then need to explore the Bible to find out what the Bible says about such an issue. You will need to check if there is a specific command or general principle that touches on the issue under your consideration. For example, it is a command in the Bible that you must not use double standards in dealing with people. If your decision will involve the use of double standards, the position of God according to the Bible is clear. Just follow it.

Alternatively, in some situations the mind of God about certain issues is expressed through the lives of people in the Bible. We are meant to learn by their examples, either good or bad. For example, in order to teach men that marrying many wives is not good for them, God included in the Bible King Solomon's experience of marrying many women. It didn't turn out well! These women turned his heart away from God and were later condemned by God. If your decision is about polygamy, the mind of God is clearly demonstrated using the lives of Bible characters to express His wisdom on this issue. Do not marry more than one wife because in the Bible polygamy always has bad results, which is a clear indication that God does not want you to be polygamous.

We can learn so much from studying the lives of Bible characters who had to make decisions on specific issues, similar to our own. For example, from studying Joseph in Genesis 39 we can see how he handled the temptation from Mrs Potiphar. You can do what he did, if you find yourself in a similar circumstance.

In contrast, the Bible also teaches God's general principles for life. These apply not just to a specific decision but also to many different issues in life, and your response needs to be obedience to these principles. For example, it is a principle that whatever a man sows he will reap, according to Galatians 6:7. So, you need to ask yourself what kind of harvest your decision will reap. If it will cause bad things for others, then you should not take this route, as it is most likely to be selfish. It is a principle for all time and all places and is not subject to our interpretation, culture or personal opinion.

If you are unable to find a relevant instruction, example or principle in the Bible, it is possible you haven't looked hard enough! The Bible's principles in particular are relevant to so many aspects of life. But there are certain more trivial choices where our decisions are not specifically right or wrong, and for these the Bible does not give any guidance. God leaves these to our personal preferences, but if you have any doubt as to whether something is right, you need to ask the Holy Spirit for specific guidance.

For example, your decision as to what colour jacket to wear today or what breakfast cereal to eat is unlikely to be found in the Bible! This kind of decision is relatively unimportant. But whenever you feel worried or anxious about a choice, or if your conscience is saying that there is something wrong here, then you need the Holy Spirit to reveal to you specifically what to do.

> 1 John 2:27: *"But the anointing which ye have received of him abided in you, and ye need not that any man teach you: but as the same anointing teaches you of all things, and is truth, and is no lie, and even as it hath taught you, ye shall abide in him."*

This verse reveals that the Holy Spirit is a teacher. You will need to ask Him what to do about issues that are not clearly stated as either right or wrong in the Bible. It will be your personal revelation, not general.

3. Meditation

> Psalm 119:15: *"I will meditate in thy precepts, and have respect unto thy ways."*

After you have been able to clarify the position of God using the Bible, it is time to meditate on the revelation you have obtained. This is time to learn how to listen to the Holy Spirit speaking to your spirit. During meditation, you will be able to sift and purify your thoughts about all you have read in the Bible. You will also gain better understanding about every message you have received through study of the Bible.

You will then need to write thoughts down as you received them through the illumination of the Holy Spirit.

4. Waiting on the Lord

Now be attentive for divine guidance about the way forward as regards your decision. It's one thing to make a decision, but implementing it is another. It can sometimes be very difficult. During your time of waiting you should expect God to speak to you clearly in one or more ways (study the next chapter on listening to His voice).

5. Prayer

After you have received guidance about your decision, you will then need to plan how you are going to put it into practice. Cover this in prayer. In 1 Samuel 16, Samuel was on a mission to choose a new king for Israel. He was told by God to go to the house of Jesse to anoint one of his children, but Samuel was not told which of the children to anoint. When Samuel reached Jesse's house, God led him step by step. The children of Jesse came before Samuel one by one until David had to be called in from where he was looking after the sheep. Sometimes, you can receive more than one option from God during all your spiritual exercises, but you need to choose the best among the good options you have. Prayer will help you to narrow down all your options to a specific one.

6. Counselling

Sometimes you need guidance from another Christian who is more experienced than you in walking with God, or in the issue that you are dealing with. Counselling and advice from such an experienced person is vital. It will help you to understand what God is really saying to you through all the revelation you have received. In 1 Samuel 3, Samuel needed the experience of the Prophet Eli to be able to understand that it was God calling him. Sometimes God has spoken to you but you did not perceive it. The advice of an experienced Christian will give you a better understanding.

GUIDANCE FROM HIS VOICE

To make good and wise decision will require that you are able to hear the voice of God when He speaks to you. God wants to guide you in decision-making but it is your responsibility to hear Him when He speaks to you. The success of your decision-making depends greatly on your ability to hear God clearly. In this chapter, we shall examine how God speaks to His children and why you don't hear God when He speaks to you.

God speaks in different ways including the following:

A. Dreams and visions

> Job 33:14-16: *"For God speaketh once, yea twice, yet man perceiveth it not. In a dream, in a vision of the night, when deep sleep falleth upon men, in slumberings upon the bed; then he openeth the ears of men, and sealeth their instruction…"*

God can speak to us either by a dream in our sleep or a vision while we're awake. A vision could be like watching a video movie in our mind's eye, or a single picture. When God sends you instruction through a dream or a vision, write it down and seek the help of mature Christians to understand what God is saying. It is wise to wait on the Lord for the correct interpretation of your dream or vision rather than to make assumptions, and to ascertain that it really is of God. You must know that dreams do not come only from God, but also from the devil, though most will simply be from your mind. That is why you should seek the face of God to be sure that your dream is from God.

B. Chastisement

God can speak to you through correction or punishment. For example, the negative consequences of something you did could be a message from God to avoid certain things.

> Hebrews 12:5-7: *"And ye have forgotten the exhortation which speaketh unto you as unto children, My son, despise not thou the chastening of the Lord, nor faint when thou art rebuked of him: For whom the Lord loveth he chasteneth, and scourgeth every son whom he receiveth. If ye endure chastening, God dealeth with you as with sons; for what son is he whom the father chasteneth not?"*

It is important to state that God's chastisement is intended for your good and to give you guidance, and it is motivated by love. Therefore, you must know that God will not chastise you in a way that contradicts His principles. He will not chastise you with sickness, poverty and curses because all these have been destroyed in your life through the birth, life, death and resurrection of Jesus Christ. Therefore do not accept or believe the devil when he tells you that your sickness or poverty or curse is from God to chastise you. It is a lie from the pit of hell to hinder you from rising against your affliction. God can chastise you through different trials, but not to work against the work of redemption He has done through Jesus Christ. God will never do anything that contradicts what He has done through Jesus.

C. A servant of God

During your decision-making, be on the lookout for God to speak to you through any of His servants.

> Hebrews 1:1: *"God, who at sundry times and in divers manners spake in time past unto the fathers by the prophets..."*

God can speak to you through any man or woman of God. It could be a Christian close to you or someone you have never met. During your decision-making, be on lookout for a divine message through any fellow Christian, particularly those with the gift of prophecy. In many situations of my life, God has confirmed His purpose in my life through a word from other men of God. The same thing can happen to you if you are sensitive to the Spirit.

D. Created things

God may decide to give you divine guidance through nature. He can speak to you through any of His works. In Genesis 15:5, God spoke to Abraham through the stars, while in Luke 12:24 Jesus spoke to the disciples using ravens. As you are looking forward to God giving you guidance, be attentive and do not rule out any possible means He may choose to speak to you.

E. Fellow human beings

God may decide to speak to you through friends, relatives, your spouse, etc.

> Deuteronomy 17:6: *"At the mouth of two witnesses, or three witnesses, shall he that is worthy of death be put to death; but at the mouth of one witness he shall not be put to death."*

There was a time I was about to implement a decision, but I was expecting God to give me confirmation of it. Before the end of the day two people walked up to me and made similar statements that exactly confirmed my decision. God can speak to you through different mouths. Be alert.

F. Talents and gifts

God can speak to you through the talents and gifts He has deposited in you. The presence of a unique ability in you is a message from God about His plan for your life. In Matthew 25:15-16, the master gave the talents to his servants without further instruction about what they should do with them. He expected them to perceive his instruction through the talents he gave them. The presence of certain abilities in you could be an indication of the call of God upon your life. With ability, comes the opportunity to practice that ability.

I was a member of a certain Pentecostal church and one day, the Pastor called me as an elder to preach on one of the Sundays. That was the first time I preached to a congregation. Afterwards, people started congratulating me for the message. From that time, it became a regular thing for the Pastor to allow me to preach. From this opportunity I was able to discover my gifting in the ministry.

G. Divine inspiration

God can speak to you through His Spirit, whom He has deposited inside you.

> Job 32:8: *"But there is a spirit in man: and the inspiration of the Almighty giveth them understanding."*

As you expect divine guidance, listen to the inspiration of the Holy Spirit – a silent voice that speaks within you. It is advisable that when you are taking an important decision that you spend time with God alone. During this quiet time, the Holy Spirit can speak clearly to your spirit. To perceive the silent voice of the Holy Spirit will require that you put yourself in a silent place, with the faith to believe that you will hear from the Spirit of God.

H. Circumstances of life

God can pass a message to you through an arrangement of the circumstances around you.

For example, God may allow you to be rejected from a place because He is taking you to a better place, which would have been impossible if you were not rejected in your present place.

In Genesis 24:13-14, the servant of Abraham prayed to God to arrange the circumstances to give him divine guidance about his journey. God did it for him. During the period of your decision-making, do not ignore every circumstance you find around you. It could be God speaking to you.

When I was living in Lesotho, Southern Africa, I worked as a teacher and my wife was also a teacher in another school. After some time, the school I was working for chose to terminate my employment. This forced me to start searching for another teaching job. But one day God spoke to me that I should stop searching for a job. This made me stop leaving home early in search of a teaching job.

During this short period I would always drop my wife at her school where she was teaching using my car. After doing this for about two weeks, the principal of the school where my wife was working saw me dropping my wife at school and asked my wife why I was not going to work. My wife told her that I had lost my teaching job and that I was looking for another post. The principal invited me to come and see her. The woman gave me a teaching job immediately. Then I realised that God had told me to stop searching for work so as to create the opportunity for me to be seen by this principal. God can speak to us through the circumstances of life.

I. Burden of the heart

God can speak to you by creating a burden in your heart – a desire, feeling or thought that refuses to go away. The thought could even grow so strong that it becomes irresistible for you.

In Nehemiah 1:1-4, Nehemiah had a burden to rebuild the walls of Jerusalem. He could not ignore the burden; he had to yield to it. Be alert when you suddenly have a burden that grows strongly inside of you. It could be God speaking to you about a decision you are about to make.

There was a time I had a burden to visit a couple and counsel them but I refused to do so. The reason why I did not yield to the burden was because the couple looked happy and there was no indication that there could be any friction in their marriage. But surprisingly I later heard that this couple had divorced. It was then I realised that I had made a mistake. If I had yielded to the burden in my heart and visited them for counselling, it might have saved their marriage. Never ignore a burden; it could be that God wants to use you to save lives.

J. Conviction of the Holy Spirit

God the Holy Spirit may convict you about something you have said or done. In such a situation, you must surrender totally to the voice of the Holy Spirit. You will find that any defensive argument is useless. Sometime such conviction comes with weeping because you totally accept your error. You are fully aware of your situation. No more arguments or self-justification.

In Acts 2:38-41, those who were convinced by the Holy Spirit through Peter's sermon totally surrendered to God. When the Holy Spirit brings you a conviction, do not resist. Just surrender and make the right decision in line with the conviction.

K. An audible voice

God can give you direction through an audible voice. You can hear a word behind you clearly and when you look back you can't see anyone. It may be God speaking to you for guidance.

> Isaiah 30:21: *"And thine ears shall hear a word behind thee, saying, This is the way, walk ye in it, when ye turn to the right hand, and when ye turn to the left."*

Be attentive when you are trusting God to lead you in your decision-making. A brother attended a party and while the event was going on, he heard a voice that told him to leave the place now. He yielded to the voice and left. Shortly after his departure a gunman came into the place threatening to shoot the people. Never ignore the audible voice of guidance from God.

L. Peace of heart

God can give you guidance by giving you peace in the heart.

> Isaiah 26:3: *"Thou wilt keep him in perfect peace, whose mind is stayed on thee: because he trusteth in thee."*

God can send peace into your heart concerning your decision. You can simply have peace about it. It means God has spoken. Conversely, a troubled heart could be an indication of God's disapproval of your purpose.

I once wanted to embark on a project but had very few resources, yet because I had peace over it I forged ahead. Miraculously there was a supply of resources. But if I had not yielded to the peace of God over the situation, I would not have known that God would supply my needs despite my initial lack of resources.

M. His Word

God may speak to you as you study the Bible, trusting God to minister to you. Certain Bible verses or stories or characters can just refuse to depart from your heart after reading them. It could be that God is calling your attention to a particular part of Scripture, to study it thoroughly for guidance. If so, there will be a message in it for you regarding your decision.

> Daniel 9:2: *"In the first year of his reign I Daniel understood by books the number of the years, whereof the word of the LORD came to Jeremiah the prophet, that he would accomplish seventy years in the desolations of Jerusalem."*

Daniel received guidance through the study of God's Word. There was a time when I had a dream where I heard a voice telling me about a particular chapter in the Bible. When I woke up, I started reading that chapter and suddenly there was a verse that grabbed my attention. I started exploring the meaning of this verse in detail and I received various revelations from this single Bible verse. It later led me into a miracle.

To avoid missing what God is saying to you, you will need to build your relationship with God. The closer to God you are, the easier it will be for you to understand His message to you. As you grow in your relationship with God, you will gain more understanding about His ways and manner of speaking to His children. But remember the importance of patience when it comes to receiving divine guidance.

We perceiveth it not

Job 33:14: *"For God speaketh once, yea twice, yet man perceiveth it not."*

God speaks to us in many ways to give us guidance in our decision-making but unfortunately we don't always perceive it. Many Christians lose vital divine guidance because they are not aware of it. The good news is that; if you know the common pitfalls regarding communication with God, you need not miss revelational knowledge from Him.

The reasons we don't perceive it when God speaks to us include the following:

1. Impatience

God speaks bit by bit in some situations and you will need patience to be able to receive the whole message that may come to you piece by piece.

Isaiah 28:13: *"But the word of the LORD was unto them precept upon precept, precept upon precept; line upon line, line upon line; here a little, and there a little…"*

God does not give all the details at once. He may choose to send you guidance little by little. Therefore, be patient and keep waiting until you receive every bit of the message that will help your decision-making. When you come into the presence of God or wait for His guidance, you will need to learn how to tarry (wait) in His presence.

2. Lack of passion

Your passion creates a fire inside of you that will cause the Holy Spirit to bring you revelation from God. If you are dull in spirit, it will be hard for your spirit to receive guidance from the Spirit of God. Your passion creates interest and a willingness to hear from God. Without passion, there will be no spark from your spirit to be ignited by the Holy Spirit.

Matthew 13:15 tells us that some people are spiritually dull of hearing. Such people can hear God's Word, yet not perceive it or understand it due to their deafness of heart. In 1 Samuel 3:16-18, Eli heard the judgement God had decreed against his home but showed no passion about it. This robs him of the opportunity to influence God's decisions. God will not continue to show you things when you show no interest. Therefore, when you are making a decision, passionately wait for God to show you further guidance and direction. In order to demonstrate your passion for divine guidance, purposely ask God for guidance, worship and praise God and declare Him as the God who gives guidance, and come into His presence with the desire to hear from Him.

3. A discouraged heart

A discouraged heart is usually negative and demotivated. When a discouraged heart hears God speaking, he will not be able to perceive it because his mental alertness is very poor. When you approach God with a discouraged heart, you may not be able to perceive what He is telling you, and even if you are able to perceive it, you are not likely to appreciate it.

In Numbers 11:10-23, Moses came before God with a discouraged heart and while God was telling him that He would provide meat for the people to eat in the desert, Moses started doubting God. A discouraged heart is not active in alertness and awareness.

> 1 Samuel 30:6: *"And David was greatly distressed; for the people spake of stoning him, because the soul of all the people was grieved, every man for his sons and for his daughters: but David encouraged himself in the LORD his God."*

In this incident, David was greatly discouraged and sorrowful because enemies had taken away his family and possessions. But in this situation David has to make an important decision – whether to pursue those criminals or not. Before David started making an inquiry from God, he first dealt with his discouraged heart by encouraging himself in the Lord. It is difficult to hear God clearly when your heart is discouraged. Therefore, if you are expecting divine guidance, you will need to first deal with any sign of discouragement in your heart. When waiting on God for guidance, if your heart is heavily discouraged, it will hinder your perception of God's voice.

4. A choked mind

You are likely to lose revelation when your mind is full up with other things. A choked mind is fully occupied and has no further space to accommodate messages from God.

In Matthew 13:7-22, Jesus revealed that if we are filled with all the cares and issues of this world, we will have no space for God to work in our hearts and lives. When your mind is choked with a series of thoughts that emanate from yourself or those around you, it is difficult to perceive any word or guidance from God. Also, in our digital age, we are bombarded with media messages and can easily suffer from information overload.

Therefore, if you are waiting on the Lord for guidance over an important decision, you will need to do some mind-clearing by removing every unnecessary distraction from your life. If you are to approach God, you need a mind with a large space to receive whatever God speaks or directs.

A lady came to our church one day and I had a discussion with her after the service. I discovered that the big issue in her life was referred to in the sermon for that day, but unfortunately she could not remember a single word of the sermon. According to her, her mind was choked up with a series of other thoughts during the service. Do not come to God with a choked mind, otherwise, you will miss a lot of helpful revelation.

5. Familiarity

Many Christians get so used to the manner in which God has spoken to them in the past that they find it strange to accept that the same God can speak to them in other ways. So, if God speaks to such Christians in a different way, they miss out.

If you don't want to miss divine guidance, avoid getting complacent about the ways in which God speaks. This familiarity with God's previous methods probably contributed to the downfall of Moses. In Exodus 17:6, God told Moses to hit the rock with his rod for people to get water. But in Numbers 20:10-11, due to emotional instability caused by anger, Moses hit the rock just as before, despite being instructed by God to just speak to the rock this time. This familiarity brought an end to the ministry of Moses.

God might have been speaking to you for many years using certain means, but never get so used to them that you are not open to other ways God speaks. He may decide to use another means at any time, without consulting you. Many people don't perceive God when He speaks to them because they have got stuck in a rut, assuming God will always do things in a certain way because that's the way it has happened in the past. Such people limit God's Spirit and are unable to perceive it when God speaks in a new way. They think it can't be God speaking if it doesn't fit with their preconceptions, but they are wrong.

6. Resentment

Resentment is to develop bitterness or lack of respect towards somebody. It makes you negative towards that person. If God decides to speak to you through the person you resent, you are likely to ignore it or disbelieve it.

In Numbers 12:1-14, Miriam and Aaron show resentment towards Moses. When God judged them, the intercession of Moses for them did not work, at least not immediately. When you resent a person in your heart, if the person intercedes for you, God will not listen.

You will be putting yourself in a very tight corner and at great risk if you operate in resentment, especially towards the people God has chosen to have spiritual authority over you. You will miss out on a lot of divine guidance and support if you resent those God has placed over you for spiritual direction.

Some years ago, God directed me to speak to a lady in our church to give her an instruction that she was not to violate. The lady was not interested, and she demonstrated a negative attitude towards me. Shortly after that, the lady violated the instruction God had given to me for her. The consequence of her action still lives with this lady up to this day.

7. A natural mind

God is supernatural and whoever wants to speak to Him must relate to Him with the mind of the supernatural – an unnatural mind. God lives in the supernatural and He speaks in supernatural ways. If you don't want to miss out on divine guidance, you will need to step up from your natural place to the supernatural level.

> Romans 4:17: *"(As it is written, I have made thee a father of many nations,) before him whom he believed, even God, who quickeneth the dead, and calleth those things which be not as though they were."*

God refers to things that do not physically exist as if they have been in existence for a long time, because he is going to call those things into being. This is unnatural to the human mind and only a mind submitted to the Holy Spirit can perceive it.

> 1 Corinthians 2:14: *"But the natural man receiveth not the things of the Spirit of God: for they are foolishness unto him: neither can he know them, because they are spiritually discerned."*

When God begins to refer to things which do not exist as if they do exist, you will need to operate in the supernatural in order to comprehend it. This means having a mind open to the miracles and the wonders of God, and a heart willing to trust Him when He tells you to do something that seems impossible, like starting a project without the resources needed. With God, natural processes can be suspended or overruled. That is unnatural, but with God, all things are possible.

8. Pre-emptiveness

This is to walk in anticipation because you foresee a possibility yourself, without having heard God on the issue. This attitude is not the same as faith – it is presumption. It will make you pre-empt God, forecasting His possible action concerning your situation. As a result, you will miss real divine guidance because of your own imagination.

In 2 Kings 5:10-14, Naaman was very angry with Elisha because he offered Naaman a solution that he did not expect. This is what Naaman said: *"Behold, I thought, He will surely come out to me, and stand, and call on the name of the LORD his God, and strike his hand over the place, and recover the leper."*

Naaman was disappointed because what he envisaged did not come to pass. He nearly missed his miracle, and would have done had it not been for his servants (verse 13), who persuaded him to obey the instruction from the man of God.

Many people have missed their divine direction because God did not come through in their situation as they have envisaged. Irrespective of your experience in dealing with God, do not predict His guidance in your decision-making. Do not assume He will work in the way you expect Him to.

9. Lack of silence

You may not be able to perceive what God is telling you because of your lack of silence and stillness. God speaks to us through His Spirit in a silent voice that only those who listen attentively will be able to hear. This calls for quiet times before God, when you stop everything else to listen to Him.

> Psalm 46:10: *"Be still, and know that I am God: I will be exalted among the heathen, I will be exalted in the earth."*
>
> Isaiah 41:1: *"Keep silence before me, O islands; and let the people renew their strength: let them come near; then let them speak: let us come near together to judgment."*

When you speak to God, expect God to also speak to you. You will need to be silent before Him in order to hear what He is saying. If you are looking to God for guidance, maintain a calm mind without agitation. Separate yourself unto God for a certain period and have a quiet time with Him, with the intention of receiving His guidance. The voice of the Spirit of God is a still small voice that can only be perceived by a quiet mind in a quiet place.

10. Lack of knowledge of His ways

You may be reading the Bible but still lack the necessary knowledge because you do not pay attention to the message relevant to your decision-making. One of the reasons why we read the Bible is to understand God and His ways of doing things. The Bible shows us how God guides His people. It also shows us the principles of how God operates.

> Psalm 103:7: *"He made known his ways unto Moses, his acts unto the children of Israel."*

This verse states that God made His ways known not just to Moses, the great leader, but to all the people of Israel. We don't have to be a theologian or great preacher to understand God's ways. God has revealed them to us through His Word. It reveals how God works out His purpose and what He will do and what He will not do.

When you study the Bible with the expectation that God will speak to you, try to focus on understanding His ways. Study how He achieved His purposes in the lives of Bible characters. Look how He fulfilled dreams and visions He gave to His people. Study how He orchestrated deliverance for His people and how He fought for them. All these will educate you about how God works. With such knowledge, you will be able to know if it is God leading you or the devil or yourself or fellow human beings. God has ways of doing things. Understand His ways and you will never lose His guidance during decision-making.

11. Sins

Sin is every kind of unrighteousness. It is impossible to enjoy divine guidance during decision-making when you dwell in sin. Sin will prevent you from hearing when God speaks to you. Sin builds a barrier between man and God.

> Isaiah 59:1-2: *"Behold, the LORD's hand is not shortened, that it cannot save; neither his ear heavy, that it cannot hear: But your iniquities have separated between you and your God, and your sins have hid his face from you, that he will not hear."*

Where there is a sin, there will be walls of separation between us and God. These walls will hinder our smooth communication with Him. If you lack divine guidance in your decision-making, it may be because of sin. Look at your life and see if there is any sin to repent of and be forgiven.

12. Build up yourself

> Jude 1:20: *"But ye, beloved, building up yourselves on your most holy faith, praying in the Holy Ghost."*

To build yourself up in the holy faith, you need to continually be filled with more of the anointing of the Holy Spirit. Pray in the Spirit by regularly speaking in tongues and spend time in worship and praise. God instructs us through His Holy Spirit who lives within us. So if you want to be able to perceive God whenever He speaks to you, you will need to be constantly filled with the Holy Spirit. Pray daily for the Spirit's anointing, regularly study the Bible and confess God's promises into your situation. Do not ignore the importance of regular fasting to subdue the flesh and exalt your spirit. Build up yourself to sharpen the line of communication between yourself and God.

Similarly, it is important for you to draw closer to God so that you have a deep relationship with Him.

> James 4:8: *"Draw nigh to God, and he will draw nigh to you. Cleanse your hands, ye sinners; and purify your hearts, ye double minded."*

As you get closer to God, so He will get closer to you. Draw closer to God in holiness, regular Bible study, services to God and others, and maintain a life of prayer and fasting. All these spiritual exercises will put you in good shape to hear God when He speaks to you.

THE RED FLAGS!

If you are not totally sure if your decision is correct biblically, there are red flags that will be a warning signal to you. If you observe any of these red flags in your decision, it's a warning that the decision you are about to make is likely to be wrong in some way. Then you will need to revisit your decision and make the right choice or choices.

It should be noted that observing any of these red flags may not necessarily imply that your decision is completely wrong, but it may mean that you need to take extra caution as you progress with your decision, or that you need to adjust it.

1. If it contradicts a biblical standard

If you observe that part of your decision appears contradictory to a biblical standard, you will need to revisit your decision and the whole process that led you into such a decision. If part of your decision contradicts what the Bible clearly says, then, it is clearly not the will of God, but you need to check that you have understood the relevant Bible passage correctly.

> Deuteronomy 28:14: *"And thou shalt not go aside from any of the words which I command thee this day, to the right hand, or to the left, to go after other gods to serve them."*

Any slight deviation from the Bible is not permitted. When you notice such a deviation in any part of your decision, you will need to change it to conform to God's will.

2. If it will advance unbelief

If your decision will result in the promotion or support of unbelief, it is very unlikely to be of God. A decision that aids atheism, encourages doubt or leads people away from the truth is not of God.

In Genesis 3:6, Adam and Eve ate the forbidden fruit and their eyes were opened as promised by Satan. Though they got the result they desired, it glorified unbelief and had tragic consequences for the whole human race. If the result of your decision would glorify an act of unbelief, it can't be from God. Even if it seems as if you have achieved your desired result, there will be a price tag that will stain it.

3. If it will produce a bad report

If you see that the outcome of your decision will give a negative impression of the Gospel of Jesus Christ, it is a red flag warning for you to exercise caution and revisit your decision. The testimony of your decision should not defame the Gospel of Jesus Christ.

> 2 Corinthians 6:3: *"Giving no offence in any thing, that the ministry be not blamed."*

You should avoid any act that will make the world speak evil of the Gospel.

4. If it troubles your conscience

If you notice that the decision you are about to make or have already made is troubling your conscience, it may be a signal from the Holy Spirit that there is something wrong with your decision. If you have no peace or rest of mind concerning your decision, you will need to pause and make a correction.

> 1 John 3:21: *"Beloved, if our heart condemn us not, then have we confidence toward God."*

This verse implies that if your heart condemns you, then something is wrong and it needs to change. Continual restlessness of the heart towards a decision could be an error warning – a red flag.

5. If your motive is wrong

If you can ascertain that the motive behind your decision was wrong according to the Bible, then, it is a signal that your decision could have been wrong. Sometimes God overrules our faults to direct things according to His will, and we can sometimes make the right decision for the wrong reasons, but generally speaking, a wrong motive means a wrong decision.

Before any decision, you must ask yourself a major question: why do I want to make this decision? Sometimes, the decision may seem right, but because the motive behind it was wrong, then there is a need for caution, because the decision usually turns out to be wrong in the end.

> Proverbs 16:2: *"All the ways of a man are clean in his own eyes; but the LORD weigheth the spirits."*

The motive behind an action is more important in God's eyes than the action itself.

6. If there is a possibility of committing sin

If your decision leads you to commit sin, it is not a right decision, and decisions that need a sinful act in order to implement them can't be of God. For example, a decision that will require forgery or manipulation in order to succeed cannot be of God.

> James 1:13: *"Let no man say when he is tempted, I am tempted of God: for God cannot be tempted with evil, neither tempteth he any man."*

God will not bless a decision that requires a sinful act for it to be established.

However, it is not impossible that during the implementation of your God-given decision, you will face temptation. In fact, such a temptation may well imply that the devil is trying to prevent your course of action because your decision is of God. And God will always provide a way for you to defeat it, as 1 Corinthians 10:13 says: *"There hath no temptation taken you but such as is common to man: but God is faithful, who will not suffer you to be tempted above that ye are able; but will with the temptation also make a way to escape, that ye may be able to bear it."*

God will always provide a way of escape from temptation, so if you find yourself under pressure to do wrong things while carrying out your God-given decision, look for God's escape route.

7. If your decision might harm other people

If your decision will bring injury to a fellow human being, it is a signal that you need to have caution and revisit your decision. It is unlikely that God will guide you into a decision that brings destruction on a fellow human being.

There are exceptions to this rule, for example in the course of a just war when good has to defeat evil, but in the vast majority of cases, God does not sanction decisions that cause harm.

> Luke 9:54-56: *"And when his disciples James and John saw this, they said, Lord, wilt thou that we command fire to come down from heaven, and consume them, even as Elias did? But he turned, and rebuked them, and said, Ye know not what manner of spirit ye are of. For the Son of man is not come to destroy men's lives, but to save them. And they went to another village."*

Jesus rebuked James and John for asking for a decision to bring destruction on those who despised Jesus. Decisions that promote suffering and damage fellow human beings are very unlikely to be of God.

8. If it has the appearance of evil

When your decision looks like evil to the outside world, you will need a serious rethink of your decision. It is possible for your decision to be right and still appear wrong to those outside the kingdom of God, but if other people are questioning the morality of your decision, then caution will be needed. Any decision that will bring you condemnation needs to be handled with caution.

1 Thessalonians 5:22 says we must *"abstain from all appearance of evil"*. The appearance of evil may not necessarily mean that the whole of your decision is evil, as people can misunderstand the works of God, but it should make you stop and think. Even if what we are doing is right, we should try to do it in such a way that doesn't bring criticism and dishonour.

For example, a decision that necessitates talking to someone of the opposite sex on your own, with no one else present, could be misinterpreted. Even though you had no evil intentions, nevertheless such an act implies a lack of wisdom and sensitivity, and leaves you vulnerable to false rumours. A decision that could compromise your good reputation should be handled with serious caution. It is not only about being right, but being wise and sensitive.

9. If it may rob you of liberty

If your decision might take away your liberty, you will need caution. For example, addiction is an enslaving habit and it can't be of God that any of His children should be enslaved in any form or manner. Any decision that brings you into captivity cannot be of God.

> 2 Corinthians 3:17: *"Now the Lord is that Spirit: and where the Spirit of the Lord is, there is liberty."*

If your decision risks robbing you of your God-given liberty, you will need to pray very well, to be doubly sure that you are not acting in error.

10. If it contradicts your basic, common experience

A decision that will contradict your basic life experience needs caution. If your decision entails specialising in a task that deviates from your life experience, you need to give it careful consideration.

For example, if your decision is to study a particular course that is totally new to you and not in line with or building on your previous knowledge, you need to ensure that it is God who is actually leading you. A decision that takes you out of your familiar world into unfamiliar territory needs caution and certainty that you are acting rightly. This is because sometimes, decisions can be subtly influenced by external factors or impure motives you are not aware of.

For example, your decision to study a particular course may be because your friends are succeeding in it, but that doesn't necessarily mean it is right for you. You might be wrongly influenced by peer pressure, or even envy. It is possible for God to lead you into such a situation that is completely new to you, but you will need to ensure that it is really God that is leading and you are not being led astray by ungodly factor(s) or agent(s).

> Ecclesiastes 4:4: *"Again, I considered all travail, and every right work, that for this a man is envied of his neighbour. This is also vanity and vexation of spirit."*

It is possible to develop ambition based on what you see in the lives of people around you, rather than on what God is saying.

11. If it is a product of negative circumstances

Sometimes, a decision can be made on the basis of negative experiences of life. Such bad experiences could be frustration, oppression, depression, hardship, joblessness, offence, fear, etc. People make decisions when they face uncertainty or discomfort, and a decision made under such pressure can often be a bad decision. We make better decisions when we are calm and in control of our emotions. Usually, emotions are involved in negative life experiences and we will be vulnerable to a decision born out of emotion rather than the leading of the Holy Spirit.

It is therefore important that we take extra caution when we are taking a decision under such negative circumstances of life. We must ensure that it is the Spirit of God that is leading us, not our desperation, distress, anger, etc.

> James 1:20: *"For the wrath of man worketh not the righteousness of God."*

Your negative emotions can rob you of working in the purposes of God. Find peace in Him before making big decisions.

12. If it involves secrecy

It is possible that your decision will involve a lot of secrecy, and sometimes that is justified, but you must ensure that you are not under demonic manipulation when doing so. Satan likes people to act secretly so that he can more easily manipulate them and isolate them from receiving the help that could open their eyes of understanding.

When you have to keep every bit of your decision secret or you are told not to let anybody know, handle it with caution. When Satan is scheming against people he will encourage them to keep it secret. This is to prevent them from receiving the intervention that could deliver them from his deception.

> Mark 4:22: *"For there is nothing hid, which shall not be manifested; neither was any thing kept secret, but that it should come abroad."*

A decision kept secret will come out in public, sooner or later. If you are under Satan's manipulation and you keep your situation secret, when the result is fully developed, it will be known to people. Be particularly cautious if you have to keep your decision secret even from those who love you most.

13. It has to be done hastily

If your decision has to be carried out quickly, take caution. If your decision does not give you enough time to think it through, you need to be sure it is right. It is true that some decisions require urgency, but you will need to approach the matter with great care.

> Proverbs 19:2: *"Also, that the soul be without knowledge, it is not good; and he that hasteth with his feet sinneth."*

Things done quickly have a greater possibility for error, hence, the famous saying: "Act in haste; repent at leisure."

14. If it has irreversible consequences

There are some decisions that cannot be changed later if proven to be wrong. In such situations, take caution before implementation. It is possible that it is God; leading you, but still approach the matter with wisdom and care.

> Hebrews 12:16-17: *"Lest there be any fornicator, or profane person, as Esau, who for one morsel of meat sold his birthright. For ye know how that afterward, when he would have inherited the blessing, he was rejected: for he found no place of repentance, though he sought it carefully with tears."*

Esau took a hasty decision but later realised his error. He tried to reverse it but it was too late.

15. If it contradicts personal prophecy

When your decision is in contradiction to a prophecy given you through another Christian, you will need to be sure that you are doing the right thing.

If you have decided to ignore the prophecy, it is probably because you don't trust the person through which the prophecy came to you, but you should still give your decision extra consideration. It is possible that you are right, but until the final outcome, nobody can be certain who is right or wrong, and God can speak through some pretty strange vessels – even donkeys (Numbers 22:28).

In Acts 21:10-14, Paul acted against a warning prophecy given to him. He wasn't being disobedient, he was acting out of his love for God. Nevertheless, the prophecy came to pass just as it was revealed. Paul was imprisoned when he came to Jerusalem as prophesied. At the end of the story, Paul came out of that prison, but the prophecy was accurate.

When your decision contradicts a prophecy, act with caution, even if you are sure that you are right.

16. If it contradicts the popular opinion of fellow Christians

It is possible that it is God leading you, despite opposition and disagreement from the crowd, but you will still need to pray to be sure. The majority is not always wrong. Sometimes, God speaks through the mouths of many people.

If you notice that almost everybody who hears about your decision criticises it, you need to take it as a warning that something may be wrong, especially if the majority of those criticising your decision are mature Christians. It is possible that God is speaking to you about your decision through the mouths of many of His children.

> Deuteronomy 19:15: *"One witness shall not rise up against a man for any iniquity, or for any sin, in any sin that he sinneth: at the mouth of two witnesses, or at the mouth of three witnesses, shall the matter be established."*

God can communicate with you through many other people. While it is true that we should not just follow the crowd, if you are sure that the crowd are following Jesus Christ and are disagreeing with you, then you should seriously ask yourself why your decision is wrong in their eyes.

17. If it raises a series of unanswered questions

If your decision has aroused a number of questions that you have no answer for, take caution. It is true that we will not know everything before embarking on our journey of faith, but if the unknowns become a burden in the heart, you will need to act with caution. It can be good to take a risk, but it must be a reasonable one. If you have a series of questions in your heart concerning your decision, it is better to seek clarification before progressing. The answers to those questions can shed more light on your decision. Avoid acting under a cloud of darkness.

> Hosea 4:6: *"My people are destroyed for lack of knowledge: because thou hast rejected knowledge, I will also reject thee, that thou shalt be no priest to me: seeing thou hast forgotten the law of thy God, I will also forget thy children."*

Ignorance leads to destruction; avoid it.

EVIDENCE OF WRONG DECISIONS

In many situations, you may not be very sure whether your decision is wright or wrong until you begin to notice the outcome of your decision. Sometimes, some decisions are so complicated that it can take years before you fully realise whether it was a right or wrong decision.

Nevertheless, there are some signs or evidence that can come your way to let you know that your decision was not right. Some of these evidences will enable you to realise that you have acted wrongly and will help you to know what steps to take, provided it is not too late.

1. Prolonged lack of inner peace

If you have taken a decision and as time goes on, you start noticing that you have no inner peace towards it, it may be a wake-up call that something was wrong in your decision.

> 2 Samuel 24:10: *"And David's heart smote him after that he had numbered the people. And David said unto the LORD, I have sinned greatly in that I have done: and now, I beseech thee, O LORD, take away the iniquity of thy servant; for I have done very foolishly."*

In this story, David counted the people of Israel despite a warning from his army commander, Joab. God was speaking through Joab to advise David not to number the people, but he did not realise it. But after David had acted wrongly in this way, his heart "smote him" – he had a troubled conscience about what he had done.

When you find yourself under a prolonged lack of inner peace concerning a recent decision, you will need to act quickly to address the matter. The Holy Spirit can cease your peace to alert you to a wrong decision.

> Romans 2:15: *"Which shew the work of the law written in their hearts, their conscience also bearing witness, and their thoughts the mean while accusing or else excusing one another…"*

As a Christian, your conscience has been activated towards God and, through the influence of the Holy Spirit, it can speak to you. If your action is wrong, your conscious can trouble you as a witness that you have gone the wrong way.

2. Lack of grace

God gives grace to enable you to pass through any trouble that may come your way, as you walk in His purpose. This grace strengthens your inner being and gives you hope in the midst of hopelessness. It also enables you to keep going, irrespective of the hindrances in your way. But a lack of grace makes you unable to cope with the challenges and forces you to quit. Without God's grace, you have no strength to move on in your decision.

God will not give you grace to execute a decision that did not originate from Him, because God can never approve of errors. God will never support a purpose that is not in line with His will. Therefore, if you notice a lack of grace upon you as a result of your decision, it may be a sign that God is not involved in your decision. The absence of God's grace makes you very vulnerable and unwilling to move on. Without God's grace, you have no internal resistance and you will notice that things are not working for you.

Philippians 4:13: *"I can do all things through Christ which strengtheneth me."*

Without God's grace, you can do nothing for His kingdom and nothing will work out well. You may need to rethink your decision if you notice a lack of divine grace.

3. Lack of supply

A decision that is not of God will not receive any backing from God. If your decision is starved of the resources it needs, such that everything fails you, it could be a sign that it is not of God. It is a biblical standard that God will always supply the resources necessary to advance His purposes, so if this is not your experience, you may need to revisit your decision.

2 Corinthians 9:8: *"And God is able to make all grace abound toward you; that ye, always having all sufficiency in all things, may abound to every good work…"*

God will supply the resources needed if a project or task is inspired by Him. If this is not your testimony, you will need to revisit your decision. It may be that the resources are delayed due to attacks of the enemy, in which case you need to pray for a breakthrough. But lack of supply may also be a sign that the work is not of God, so you will need discernment.

4. Repeated affliction

When God allows a situation to repeat itself, there is a need for urgent attention. A problem that keeps on re-occurring could be a warning signal that something urgently needs to be fixed. If you keep on suffering the same problems regarding your decision, it could be a sign that you need to make some adjustments.

In Genesis 12:10-16 and Genesis 20:1-2, Abraham twice lost Sarah to another man because of his own deception. This was a message that you can't keep on doing wrong things and expect the results to be any different.

5. Violation of God's promises

When you begin to notice an event related to your decision that contradicts the promises of God, it may be a warning that something is wrong. In Joshua 1:5, God promised Joshua that he would not lose in battle, but in Joshua 7:1-12 Joshua lost a battle. This contradicted the promise of God. It was later revealed that Joshua lost because there was a sin in the camp of Israel. When you see something happen that contradicts what God has promised you in the past, it is a wake-up call to start revisiting your decision, or see if there is something sinful in the way it is being implemented.

6. Disinheritance

This is when somebody loses what God has given to him. In Genesis 2, God gave Adam and Eve the Garden of Eden but in Genesis 3, they were driven out of the place. This is because Adam and Eve took the fruit that God had forbidden to them. They took what God did not give and lost what God did give.

In your decision implementation, if you notice that you are losing what God has given you before, it may be that you have taken what God has not given you. If your decision is opening a door to spiritual robber to steal God's blessings in your life, it may be that you have taken something that was not in God's plan for you.

7. Direct rebuke

God can make you aware of your wrong decision through a direct rebuke. He may send you somebody to rebuke you for acting wrongly. In 2 Samuel 12:1-7, Nathan rebuked David for taking the decisions to marry Bathsheba and kill her husband. In your situation, a direct rebuke can come from God either through somebody close to you or somebody distant from you. It may be during a sermon from a man of God you have never met, or personally from a close friend. It may also come to you through a dream or vision, or other gift of the Spirit. Be sensitive to the Spirit, and don't hesitate to act when God rebukes you through any channel He may choose.

8. Prolonged disunity

Continual disunity and internal disagreement between your team members could be a sign that your decision needs adjustment. In Genesis 21:9-12, a misunderstanding between Sarah and Abraham over Hagar was unmanageable and could not be resolved. This led to Hagar's departure from the home of Abraham. This showed that the decision of Abraham and Sarah to use Hagar to have a child was not of God.

When you notice a division among your team that cannot be resolved, it may be a warning that something has gone wrong not just in your team but in your decision, and there is a need for adjustment.

1 Corinthians 14:33: *"For God is not the author of confusion, but of peace, as in all churches of the saints."*

This verse states that confusion is not of God. Therefore prolonged confusion that becomes unmanageable is evidence of the absence of God's involvement.

9. Divine revelation

God may make you aware of your wrong decision by revealing to you; what went wrong through revelation. In Joshua 9:3-22, Joshua and the leaders of Israel were deceived by the Gibeonites but the deception was revealed after three days. God will not allow the secret of the enemy to forever be hidden in your situation. At a certain point, God will expose to you; where you are being deceived. This may come through personal revelation or other means.

10. God is contending with you

Sometimes, God may decide to be your problem because you have made a wrong decision. In that case, there will be no way forward. Everything will come to a standstill. Heaven will appear sealed up to you, with no prayers getting through. When you experience such a serious situation, you will need to investigate and ask God to reveal to you; where you have gone wrong.

Haggai 1:6-9: *"Ye have sown much, and bring in little; ye eat, but ye have not enough; ye drink, but ye are not filled with drink; ye clothe you, but there is none warm; and he that earneth wages earneth wages to put it into a bag with holes. Thus saith the LORD of hosts; Consider your ways. Go up to the mountain, and bring wood, and build the house; and I will take pleasure in it, and I will be glorified, saith the LORD. Ye looked for much, and, lo, it came to little; and when ye brought it home, I did blow upon it. Why? saith the LORD of hosts. Because of mine house that is waste, and ye run every man unto his own house."*

In these verses, God declared to Israel that He was their problem. He was the one devouring their resources. He was the one who hindered their fruitfulness. This was because of their wrong decision to neglect the house of God.

If you are praying and fasting and doing everything you can without making any headway, it may be that your decision has provoked God to arise against you. But be encouraged – God will return to your side if you admit your mistake, change what you were doing and ask His forgiveness.

DECISIONS IN DIVERSITIES

Not my will

In some situations, a decision may be imposed on you. In this case, you are forced to accept a particular decision without your consent and against your will.

When you find yourself in this situation, the only thing you can do is to commit yourself and the situation into the hands of God. He is able to reverse any decision and can turn it around for your own good.

> Genesis 37:27-28: *"Come, and let us sell him to the Ishmeelites, and let not our hand be upon him; for he is our brother and our flesh. And his brethren were content. Then there passed by Midianites merchantmen; and they drew and lifted up Joseph out of the pit, and sold Joseph to the Ishmeelites for twenty pieces of silver: and they brought Joseph into Egypt."*

The decision to go to Egypt was not taken by Joseph. He was sold as a slave and taken to Egypt. In this circumstance, there was nothing Joseph could do to change the situation. He could only commit himself and his future into the hands of God. In the end, God turned the situation around for Joseph. He became deputy to King Pharaoh of Egypt.

Despite any decision imposed on you, God is still in control of the situation. When you face such a difficult experience, trust God to work things out in your favour, but avoid doing anything that will complicate the situation.

> Romans 8:28: *"And we know that all things work together for good to them that love God, to them who are the called according to his purpose."*

This verse is a consolation for you, and encouragement to trust God to work for your ultimate good in every decision, both good and bad, imposed on you.

Premature decisions

A premature decision is a decision that is made too early. It should have been delayed, to give more time for consideration.

> Luke 15:11-13: *"And he said, A certain man had two sons: And the younger of them said to his father, Father, give me the portion of goods that falleth to me. And he divided unto them his living. And not many days after the younger son gathered all together, and took his journey into a far country, and there wasted his substance with riotous living."*

In this story the prodigal son asked his father for his inheritance. He did not wait for his father to willingly give him his inheritance when his father chose, nor to receive it when his father died. So the prodigal son was not yet ready to be in charge of such wealth, as the situation later proved. At the time of his decision, he lacked all the necessary skills for responsibly managing his inheritance. If he had just waited, his father would have given it to him at the right time. His father was probably waiting for him to mature to the level where he would be able to properly deal with his inheritance, and not waste it.

Some decisions come too early. Therefore, before you make a decision, ask yourself if the time is ripe for such a decision. It is also important for you to see if you have all the attributes required to make such a decision a success. A premature decision could cost you a lot; be aware.

Leaving the known for the unknown

Sometimes, your decision will mean moving from a place of certainty to uncertainty. There is always a risk involved in decisions, but some decisions involve really stepping out into the unknown. It is therefore imperative that you get your bearings right. Before you move out of the known into the unknown, be sure that you know what you are doing.

> Hebrews 11:8: *"By faith Abraham, when he was called to go out into a place which he should after receive for an inheritance, obeyed; and he went out, not knowing whither he went."*

In this story, Abraham was to leave his familiar territory for a new place that he did not know. It was very important for Abraham to be certain that it was God who was telling him to move, because the cost of this decision would have been very great if he had got it wrong.

Many Christians have shipwrecked their lives due to the 'God Says Syndrome'. This is where people get into serious trouble because they take a decision thinking that it is God instructing them, but it is clear later that they were deceived. You must be aware that your mind could get messages from different sources. The Spirit of God can speak to you but so can Satan. Your deepest emotions can also affect your decisions, leading you in a wrong direction. Be sure that you have actually heard from God before you act.

> 1 John 4:1: *"Beloved, believe not every spirit, but try the spirits whether they are of God: because many false prophets are gone out into the world."*

From this verse, it is clear that we should test the spirit that is sponsoring our decision, to see whether it is of God or not.

No decision is a decision

There are many ways people respond to situations in their lives. Some people may choose to act immediately, while others delay a decision or don't do anything at all when a crisis arises. You must be aware that whichever option you choose, it is still a decision, and there will be consequences attached to it. If your decision is to make no decision it is still a decision, and it will not exonerate you from facing the consequences of your option.

> Exodus 12:38: *"And a mixed multitude went up also with them; and flocks, and herds, even very much cattle."*

In the story of Israel's Exodus from Egypt, Israel left with other people from Egypt. This was contrary to the promise God gave to Moses in Exodus 3, when God appeared to him in the burning bush. God told Moses that He had come to take Israel out of the land of Egypt. God said nothing about a "mixed multitude" of people coming with them. But when Moses saw the variety of people following Israel out of Egypt, he did nothing to address the situation. He took no decision about it, so the people came along.

Unfortunately, Moses' decision to take no decision did not protect Israel from the negative influences of the different people who had come with them. Many Israelites died in the desert as a result.

It is important for you to know that your decision to take no decision does not free you from facing the consequences of your inaction. A problem you ignore, is a problem coming back to haunt you. Be wise. Act now, before it is too late.

Having foresight

In many situations, there are warning signals that can help you to be pro-active and take the necessary steps to prevent a problem before it fully develops. Careful observation of your situation will enable you to foresee the likely developments that will follow. This will help you to act before the impending incident occurs, perhaps establishing necessary boundaries and putting precautions into position as a safeguard.

> *Genesis 39:7-12: "And it came to pass after these things, that his master's wife cast her eyes upon Joseph; and she said, Lie with me. But he refused, and said unto his master's wife, Behold, my master wotteth not what is with me in the house, and he hath committed all that he hath to my hand; there is none greater in this house than I; neither hath he kept back any thing from me but thee, because thou art his wife: how then can I do this great wickedness, and sin against God? And it came to pass, as she spake to Joseph day by day, that he hearkened not unto her, to lie by her, or to be with her. And it came to pass about this time, that Joseph went into the house to do his business; and there was none of the men of the house there within. And she caught him by his garment, saying, Lie with me: and he left his garment in her hand, and fled, and got him out."*

This story reveals that before the wife of Potiphar attempted to force Joseph to sleep with her, she had been putting pressure upon Joseph to do so. She tried to persuade him for a long time, and Joseph had been resisting, so Joseph should have realised that it was only a matter of time before she would try to have her way. He was right to resist her advances, but he should also have taken certain steps to address the situation, like not allowing himself to be in the same room with her when no one else was around. That situation gave her the opportunity she had been waiting for. He should have foreseen that her lust would escalate into a potential rape situation if there was no one around to prevent it.

If certain events are happening around you, they can be a sign that you need to prevent a situation escalating out of control. If you can foresee that something bad is about to happen, you don't need to wait until it strikes before you take any action. Instead, make a pre-emptive decision to try to prevent the incident occurring.

For example, a little bad attitude from somebody could be a warning signal of worse to come in the future from that person. You can start putting certain boundaries around yourself as a safeguard – like avoiding contact with that person, if possible. Many problems can be avoided if we can be pro-active.

Unnecessary decisions

Some decisions are simply unnecessary. For example, you might make a decision as a result of somebody trying to use you for his/her own advantage. Such a decision will not benefit you in any way, it will only put you in bondage, unless the Lord intervenes in your favour. Therefore, before you take a decision, ask yourself if it is necessary or if it is an attempt by somebody else to manipulate you for their own purposes.

In Joshua 9:1-20, the Gibeonites came to Joshua to make a covenant with Israel so that they could live among them. The demand seems strange, but Joshua entered into a covenant with them without asking God if it was right. It was later discovered that the Gibeonites had deceived Joshua into the covenant. They had used him for their own advantage and security. The rationale behind the covenant and its demand seemed reasonable, so Joshua entered into it, not knowing that he was being used. If Joshua had chosen not to enter into such an agreement, it would not have had the negative consequences that ensued.

Before you make a decision due to pressure from someone else, ensure that it is necessary and that it will not trap you into a situation that you will not be able to escape. Some decisions are unnecessary. There is no reasonable basis for them. They will only lead to trouble that could have been avoided.

From error to error

A decision birthed in error will naturally attract more errors as it develops. The fact is, it is impossible to add an error to another error and expect a positive result. Whenever you encounter complications in your decision implementation, it is advisable to revisit your decision to see if there was a mistake made at the beginning.

In 2 Samuel 11:1-24, David was supposed to be at the battleground fighting alongside the army of Israel, but he chose to stay at home. It was a bad decision. Why? Because while relaxing in his palace, he saw the wife of Uriah bathing, was filled with lust and slept with her. That was another decision of error.

When David was told by the woman that she was now pregnant, David tried to get Uriah to sleep with her, so that he would think the baby, when born, was his. But David's trickery didn't work, so he took a decision on how to kill Uriah, and it succeeded. That was another decision of error.

David then finally chose to bring the woman into his own house and married her – another decision of error because he did not deserve to marry her because of what he had done.

So David made a series of erroneous decisions as a result of his first wrong decision. If he had gone to battle instead, he would have been in the right place at the right time, fighting alongside the army of Israel, and would never have laid eyes on a naked Bathsheba.

If the foundation of your decision is erroneous, you are likely to fall into even more errors as you take further steps. One thing leads to another – one error, if not urgently corrected, will lead to another one.

Agree to disagree

Whenever you are making a corporate decision, get ready to agree to disagree with other people.

You won't always be able to agree with everyone in making joint decisions, so you need to be able to disagree agreeably with other people. Everyone has to make their own mind up on issues, so you just have to accept that it's not always possible to persuade everyone of your point of view.

> In Acts 15:39-40 we read of a disagreement between Paul and Barnabas: *"And the contention was so sharp between them, that they departed asunder one from the other: and so Barnabas took Mark, and sailed unto Cyprus; and Paul chose Silas, and departed, being recommended by the brethren unto the grace of God."*

In this story, Paul and Barnabas could not agree on a joint decision about a missionary trip. They eventually agreed to disagree, each deciding to go their own way. Paul and Barnabas individually acted according to their own convictions. There is no indication in these verses that someone was right and someone was wrong. It was a matter of satisfying their conscience and doing what they considered right.

You won't always be able to find agreement in a team or group. You will need to be ready to go it alone, if necessary. If you and other people cannot agree on a decision, then agree to disagree and move on.

Persuasion

Decisions can often be taken not because you are very sure of the right action but because of strong persuasion by another person. The one persuading you could be very skilful in convincing other people to act in a certain way. But be aware before you yield to persuasion that you will still face the consequences of your decision, despite the fact that you have acted under inducement.

In Genesis 2, Adam and Eve chose to obey the instruction they received from God not to eat the forbidden fruit. They never disobeyed this instruction until they welcomed a stranger into their midst, who was very skilful in persuading them to do what he wanted.

> Genesis 3:1: *"Now the serpent was more subtil than any beast of the field which the LORD God had made. And he said unto the woman, Yea, hath God said, Ye shall not eat of every tree of the garden?"*

In this Bible story, Satan came to persuade Adam and Eve to disobey God and they yielded to his inducement. They shifted from their original position of obedience to God. They were convinced by the sweet tongue of Satan. They never knew they were being deceived, but they had to face the severe consequences of giving in to his persuasion.

Before you make a decision, ensure that you are not acting under the inducement of other people but from your own internal conviction. No matter how strong the opinion of another person may be, ensure that you are personally convinced before you make a decision. Do not yield to sweet talk from another person, because it may be wrong.

2 Timothy 3:13: *"But evil men and seducers shall wax worse and worse, deceiving, and being deceived."*

It is possible that the person trying to persuade you about something is unknowingly under deception themselves. They may be talking to you with boldness and assurance, but that does not mean that they are right. A person can be so deceived about something that they are fully capable of persuading others to follow them.

Alternatively, they may have a malign motive for persuading you about a particular decision. So before you change your decision due to persuasion from another person, think deeply. Be wise.

A decision to vow

A vow is a solemn promise to do a certain thing. Some people decide to make a vow when dealing with God. They vow to do certain things for Him if He will do a certain thing for them. But you can't twist God's arm in this way – He never acts under duress. He did made covenants with people in the Old Testament, but that was all under His control and at His instigation.

No matter how big your vow is, God is bigger than your vow. You must know that your vow can't force God to do what it is not already in His plan for your life. You can't bribe God to act against His righteous purpose.

> 1 Samuel 1:11: *"And she vowed a vow, and said, O LORD of hosts, if thou wilt indeed look on the affliction of thine handmaid, and remember me, and not forget thine handmaid, but wilt give unto thine handmaid a man child, then I will give him unto the LORD all the days of his life, and there shall no razor come upon his head."*

Hannah took a decision to vow before God concerning her need and God answered. But God answered not because He did not want to miss the reward of Hannah's vow, but because it was all part of promoting His divine plan. Therefore, before you make a vow, check with the Spirit of God if it is in line with the divine plan of God.

A true vow has no conditions attached. This kind of vow is a good thing, showing your determination to do what's right and obey God in some way.

Furthermore, before you choose to make a vow, ensure that you are in a position to fulfil the vow. Do not make such a serious decision out of emotion.

A vow must be honoured, even if it seems that things are not turning out as you expected or hoped. It may be a test from God to prove the genuineness of your love for Him.

There is a warning on this in Ecclesiastes 5:4-6: *"When thou vowest a vow unto God, defer not to pay it; for he hath no pleasure in fools: pay that which thou hast vowed. Better is it that thou shouldest not vow, than that thou shouldest vow and not pay. Suffer not thy mouth to cause thy flesh to sin; neither say thou before the angel, that it was an error: wherefore should God be angry at thy voice, and destroy the work of thine hands?"*

It is better not to vow at all than to make a vow that you struggle to keep.

When you can't decide

There is bound to come a time when you just can't make your mind up about a certain decision. Fortunately, we have a God who cares about every detail of our lives, and you can ask for His help to make the right decision.

> Acts 9:6: *"And he trembling and astonished said, Lord, what wilt thou have me to do? And the Lord said unto him, Arise, and go into the city, and it shall be told thee what thou must do."*

Paul, on his way to Damascus, had an encounter with God. At this stage of his life, he did not know the reason why Jesus appeared to him, other than to stop him persecuting Christians. He was confused about what God wanted him to do with his life now, because up until this time, he thought he had been doing God's will, and now he realised that he had got it all wrong.

So, Paul asked God an honest question: *"What wilt thou have me to do?"* It is the question of a person who can't decide what to do in a situation.

When you can't make a decision, be honest with yourself. Do not pretend that you know what to do. Seek help from credible people who you trust. Ask for counselling from those who are more experienced than you. Ask God to help you. Do not try to fix what you do not know how to fix.

I can't take it anymore

A decision could be a reflection of exhaustion or being fed up with a certain situation. Maybe you have permitted something to happen in your life up until now, but it is now troubling you so much that you want to get rid of it. You used to put up with it but now you have chosen not to do so anymore. It is a decision of: "I've had enough."

When you get to this juncture, you will need boldness to act with a strong determination. This is because such a situation might have developed a strong root in your life during the time you used to permit it. To now uproot a tree of strong root will require strength and determination.

If your decision is to succeed, you will need to find reasons to negate every reason you entertained before, that had allowed you to permit such a situation. To make such a decision stick will require that you are sure that you are truly tired of the situation, and that there will be no turning back or regret or reconsideration.

> Genesis 13:7-9: *"And there was a strife between the herdmen of Abram's cattle and the herdmen of Lot's cattle: and the Canaanite and the Perizzite dwelled then in the land. And Abram said unto Lot, Let there be no strife, I pray thee, between me and thee, and between my herdmen and thy herdmen; for we be brethren. Is not the whole land before thee? Separate thyself, I pray thee, from me: if thou wilt take the left hand, then I will go to the right; or if thou depart to the right hand, then I will go to the left."*

In this story Abraham had been tolerating incessant strife from Lot and his servants for a long time. Perhaps Abraham had been able to tolerate this ugly situation because he had allowed for the fact that Lot was a relative and he did not want to violate that bond. But after some time, the situation became unmanageable for Abraham and he chose not to allow it anymore. He peacefully separated from Lot.

When you get to your limit, you must be real and act accordingly.

Potential exposure

Every decision has its own potential exposure. By that; I mean that every decision has an outcome – you will be exposed to a new situation, either good or bad. It is wise to investigate the potential exposure attached to your decision.

> Luke 15:12-16: *"And the younger of them said to his father, Father, give me the portion of goods that falleth to me. And he*

divided unto them his living. And not many days after the younger son gathered all together, and took his journey into a far country, and there wasted his substance with riotous living. And when he had spent all, there arose a mighty famine in that land; and he began to be in want. And he went and joined himself to a citizen of that country; and he sent him into his fields to feed swine. And he would fain have filled his belly with the husks that the swine did eat: and no man gave unto him."

The prodigal son chose to take his inheritance and travel to a far country where nobody knew him. He did not investigate the potential exposure attached to his decision. Soon, the reality came. He found his decision exposed him to famine, lack of help, loneliness and shame. If he had thought about the potential exposure attached to his decision, he probably would have acted differently.

Before you embark on your decision, ask yourself the potential things you will be exposed to as a result of it. This will help you to know what is likely to come your way as you pursue your decision. It will also help you to be pro-active.

Never say never

There are certain decisions you will make that will tempt you to act as if you know what the future holds. In such a temptation, you may feel like closing every possible door to turning back. But wise people never say never, because you never can tell what the future holds, neither can you tell how your decision will turn out.

In Judges 11:1-10, Jephthah's brothers forced him to leave, refusing to give him his inheritance. But very soon, they discovered that they needed his help to lead them into battle against their enemies. They did not know that they would need his help again.

Before you make decision that will involve the total closing of a door, be very careful because you may find yourself needing to come back to it in the future. Never say never.

From Jerusalem to Jericho

Some decisions can be likened to a man travelling from Jerusalem to Jericho.

> Luke 10:30: *"And Jesus answering said, A certain man went down from Jerusalem to Jericho, and fell among thieves, which stripped him of his raiment, and wounded him, and departed, leaving him half dead."*

In this parable of the good Samaritan, the man travelling from Jerusalem to Jericho is attacked by robbers. What made the man make a decision to walk from Jerusalem to Jericho? Jerusalem was a place of peace and relative safety, but the road to Jericho was notorious for bandits and thieves. It was not a wise decision.

Some decisions involve moving from a place of comfort to a place of tribulation. Sometimes, people make a decision out of anger or pride and they walk out of peace and into a place of trouble, or from a place of acceptance to one of rejection, from abundance into want. Therefore, before you make a decision to leave a pleasant place in search of greener pastures, think it over very carefully, so that your situation will not be like the man who travelled from Jerusalem to Jericho and was attacked by robbers.

A decision that tempts God

Some decisions are a direct temptation of God and are therefore doomed to fail.

You will be tempting God in your decision if you willingly make a decision in order to see what God will do in such a situation. For example, you are tempting God if you willingly chose a wrong path in order to see if God will intervene. If you choose to create a difficulty for yourself in the hope that God will deliver you from it, that's an attempt to tempt God. If you willingly step into a fire knowing full well that fire can burn you, you are tempting God. In such a situation, God will not intervene.

> Numbers 14:22: *"Because all those men which have seen my glory, and my miracles, which I did in Egypt and in the wilderness, and have tempted me now these ten times, and have not hearkened to my voice..."*

These men of Israel willingly refused to act rightly despite knowing the right things to do. They chose to act in a way that would anger God despite being fully aware of their action. They chose to ignore all the warnings from God, ten times. Their actions tempted God to never punish them for their sins, but of course God could not be a holy God if he never dealt with evil. Eventually, He destroyed them in the desert.

Never tempt God in your decision. Do not make a wrong decision willingly and then start crying to God for intervention when you suffer the consequences of your decision. God is not bound to help you, even in this era of His grace, because He may need to teach you a lesson.

WHY PEOPLE MAKE WRONG DECISIONS

In reality, nobody intentionally makes faulty decisions. Every normal person wants their decision to be right and to achieve their intentions. In fact, every person believes that his or her decision is right until the outcome proves otherwise.

But unfortunately, people do unintentionally make many wrong decisions, and the natural consequence of a wrong decision is failure.

It is therefore very important to understand the factors that can lead you to make wrong decisions. If you can do this, you will be able to avoid the pitfalls in your decision-making.

In this chapter, we will examine the factors that contribute to wrong decisions. They can contaminate decisions at the outset, or during the planning stage or during implementation. Thankfully, some passages of the Bible were specifically written to help our understanding of each of these factors. If you study these Bible verses, God will help you to improve your decision-making.

So, why do we make wrong decisions? Here's my list.

1. Unbelief

Unbelief means absence of faith in God. It also means lack of trust in the Word of God. Unbelief makes a person act contrary to what God has said concerning many situations.

In Genesis 15:4, God promised Abraham a son from his own body. But in Genesis 16:1-4, due to unbelief, Sarah put pressure on Abraham to impregnate Hagar to have a child. Both Abraham and Sarah decided to stop trusting God to perform His word concerning them.

Events in the family of Abraham and Sarah later became volatile due to the presence of the child born to Abraham by Hagar. This clearly shows that their decision was wrong, because it deviated from the promise of God.

It is only a matter of time before lack of faith in God's Word will influence you to make wrong decisions. In order to avoid wrong decisions, get rid of unbelief in your heart and start trusting God's Word for direction.

(For further study, see: Psalm 106:24, Hebrews 3:12, Hebrew 4:2, Hebrews 12:15, 1 Thessalonians 2:13)

2. Shallow thinking

The inability to think deeply can cause wrong decisions. A shallow thinker does not have a deep understanding of the consequences of his actions or decisions. Such a person makes a decision on generalities instead of being specific.

In order to gain a deep understanding of your intended decision, you will need to meditate on it several times to bring illumination to your mind over the pros and cons of the decision. This will help you to see the hidden details of the decision that may prove extremely important to the outcome.

People who rush into decisions usually lack deep thinking and so have not given enough time for the Holy Spirit to reveal vital hidden facts to them.

> Judges 11:30-31: *"And Jephthah vowed a vow unto the LORD, and said, If thou shalt without fail deliver the children of Ammon into mine hands, then it shall be, that whatsoever cometh forth of the doors of my house to meet me, when I return in peace from the children of Ammon, shall surely be the LORD's, and I will offer it up for a burnt offering."*

In this story, Jephthah vowed to the Lord that he would sacrifice whatever came out of his house first after defeating the Ammonites, if God would help him defeat their army. Unfortunately, it was his only daughter that came out of his house first to greet him, celebrating his victory (Judges 11:34-35).

This was a foolish vow. Jephthah had not thought it through properly. He made a rash and uninformed promise to the Lord, knowing full well that he had no idea who or what he would first see come out of his house when he returned home.

You are likely to make wrong decisions when you act on emotion and without properly thinking over the matter before acting.

(For further study, see: James 3:2, Ecclesiastes 5:2-6, Proverbs 14:15, Psalm 119:99, Hebrews 5:12)

3. Immaturity

An immature person is one who is not yet fully grown up and is unable to handle certain things in life. This is because an immature person thinks, speaks and acts like a child, and is not yet able to properly distinguish evil from good. This is because the person has not developed their own spiritual discernment, and has not been taught to understand what is good and what is bad.

> 1 Corinthians 13:11: *"When I was a child, I spake as a child, I understood as a child, I thought as a child: but when I became a man, I put away childish things."*

The level of understanding of an immature person is low, so his decision-making will be very defective. In order not to fall into error by the decisions such a person makes, he will need to improve his understanding of what is good and bad.

> Hebrews 5:14: *"But strong meat belongeth to them that are of full age, even those who by reason of use have their senses exercised to discern both good and evil."*

The writer to the Hebrews indicates that you can't make right decisions unless you know how to discern between good and evil, because you may see evil as being good and so get your decisions wrong. 1 Corinthians 2:14 advises that in order to grow spiritually, we need to stop being natural in our thinking. We can do this by making a conscious effort to grow in the Word of God, so we are transformed by the renewing of our mind (Romans 12:12).

(For further study, see: 1 Corinthians 14:20, Ephesians 4:14, 1 Peter 2:2, 2 Peter 3:18, Hebrews 6:1)

4. Assumptions

Some people make decisions based on what they consider is right or wrong, but without finding out if what they believe has been proved to be right. Such people enter into decisions ignorant of potential dangers.

Other people have a naïve assumption that their decision will work out well, despite making no effort to ensure it will. They just assume the outcome, without any basis in evidence. None of the parameters they consider in their decision is tested for reliability. It is only a matter of time before there will be a series of negative surprises for them.

> 1 Samuel 17:39: *"And David girded his sword upon his armour, and he assayed to go; for he had not proved it. And David said unto Saul, I cannot go with these; for I have not proved them. And David put them off him."*

In this verse, after King Saul put his armour on David to face Goliath in battle, David removed it because he had not tested the armour out. David refused to operate on the assumption of Saul's recommendation for his armour. In your decision-making, avoid making choices, as much as possible, on parameters you have not tested personally. You must have personal assurance before making decisions about the facts under consideration.

It is worth stating that sometimes, under certain situations, there may be no option but to make an assumption. But it is advisable that every effort is made to minimise the risk. If you have to guess, make sure it's an educated guess.

(For further study, see: Proverbs 18:2, 1 John 4:1, John 7:24, 2 Peter 3:16-17, 2 Corinthians 10:7)

5. Religious spirit

This is the spirit that protects the old against the new. It believes in the status quo. It states that the situation must continue as it has always been. It resists new ideas.

Wrong decisions are imminent when you operate only with the old knowledge that you have about the situation in hand. If you choose to make decisions on current issues based on what you knew about it yesterday, without exploring any possible changes that might have taken place in the meantime, then you are likely to get into error. To make wise decisions, gather all relevant information both from the past and the present. Be ready to adopt change.

> Mark 2:22: *"And no man putteth new wine into old bottles: else the new wine doth burst the bottles, and the wine is spilled, and the bottles will be marred: but new wine must be put into new bottles."*

Every effort to apply what is obsolete to the new will result into great loss. Let the new go with the new.

(For further study, see: Romans 12:2, 2 Corinthians 4:4, Psalm 19:2, James 3:17-18, Ecclesiastes 3:1-3)

6. Overconfidence

It is good to have self-confidence but it is not good to be overconfident. Overconfidence can make you overlook dangerous factors in your decision-making. You may overestimate yourself when making certain decisions which may expose you to challenges beyond your capability. It is therefore very important that you practice humility in your decisions. Humbly consider every fact before making a decision and never underestimate any potential challenge. Do not underestimate your opponents.

In Joshua 7:3-4, the Israelites faced the little city of Ai with few soldiers due to overconfidence. They failed to make all the necessary preparations for the battle. They did not even bother to consult God for direction, probably because they thought the battle was not going to be difficult. They strongly believed that the people of Ai were no match for them in war. Alas, they were proved wrong. The Israelites lost the battle.

(For further study, see: Proverbs 16:18, 1 Corinthians 10:12, 2 Corinthians 13:5, Proverbs 28:26, Isaiah 47:8)

7. Bad team-playing

If you are not good at working with other people, you may be tempted to make decisions without consulting others. Some decisions benefit from including other people in the decision-making process, and you may suffer the consequences if you choose to exclude other people and make yourself the centre of all the action. If you only consider your own views, you will put upon yourself a load that is beyond your strength.

Not only that, in a team situation, you will upset other people, as they will not feel valued, and it is especially important to consult others if you are making a decision that will affect them as well as yourself.

There are many people who never include other people in their plans because they are uncomfortable with working in a team. Such people go it alone. They usually end up with failure.

Ecclesiastes 4:9-12 states that two are better than one. That is, it is better to work as a team because there will be mutual assistance. When you jointly make decisions or incorporate other people's opinions into your decision process, you will enjoy wider support and benefits. But without good team playing, you will not be able to get along with other people.

(For further study, see: Proverbs 27:17, Proverbs 18:24, Proverbs 17:17, 1 Samuel 23:16, 1 Thessalonians 5:11)

8. Tiredness

Making decisions when tired attracts misjudgement due to fatigue.

During tiredness, the mind is not in its clearest state. To make accurate decisions you need to be alert and in a sound mind.

In 1 Kings 19, shortly after a glorious victory over the prophets of Baal, Elijah fled from Jezebel and later complained to God about his ordeals. This could be explained by tiredness. Perhaps he had not rested enough from one fight before another fight came. Verse 4 certainly mentions that he lay down to sleep.

Tiredness makes your mind malfunction, it makes you want to rush decisions so that you can get some rest, and it reduces your resistance to negative emotions. All of this is bad for decision-making. Good decision-making requires that you are fresh, both mentally and psychologically.

(For further study, see: Romans 12:11, Jeremiah 31:25, Hebrews 12:12-13, Isaiah 40:28-31, Matthew 11:28-29)

9. Wrong timing

There is a right time for everything, including decision-making. Do not make a decision when you are not in the right state of mind, when you are tired, biased, angry, depressed, distracted, afraid or anxious.

For example, decision-making should not be done when you are emotional, because the choices will be controlled by emotion instead of intellect. It is intellectual strength that determines right decision-making, as well as spiritual guidance.

Similarly, decisions made during grief or while stressed are likely to be wrong. A decision whether to marry, made under the pressure that age is no longer on your side, is likely to lead to error. This is because your thoughts will be controlled by your worries about old age instead of the wisdom to make the right choice. Furthermore, the decision of what to eat when you are seriously hungry is likely to be unhealthy. The pressure of hunger controls your choice instead of your intellect.

In Genesis 25:32-34, Esau sold his birth-right to Jacob when he was desperately hungry. He later regretted it but it was too late. The wrong time to make a decision is when your mind is clouded by other needs or pressures.

(For further study, see: Ecclesiastes 3:1, 9:11, Micah 3:8, Hebrews 12:16-17, 2 Timothy 1:7)

10. Walking by sight

A person who depends solely on the physical appearance of a situation for guidance will probably make a wrong decision. This is because such a person will make choices based on what can be seen but ignore vital factors that are detected not with your eyes but with your mind and spirit, with prayer and God's Word.

In Genesis 13, Lot chose a land that appeared good and well-watered but he did not know that the choice would lead him to live among evil people. His decision was solely based on what he could see with his eyes, ignoring other factors that were either hidden or not so obvious.

Avoid making decisions based only on attractive physical appearances, because there could be hidden elements that have serious consequences. Look deeper into the situation, at issues like motives, spiritual dangers, possible deception, etc.

(For further study, see: 2 Corinthians 5:7, 5:12, 4:18, Matthew 23:27, 1 Samuel 16:7)

11. Mindset

A mindset is a belief system based on preconceived thoughts, ideas and opinions. This creates an attitude that determines how somebody will respond in any given situation. It conditions your thinking pattern.

A mindset could be positive or negative. A person of negative mindset will likely approach a situation with the mentality of impossibility, even if there is a good chance of success, while a person of a positive mindset is more likely to think things are possible – and sometimes be over-optimistic.

The problem with the mindset is that it hinders originality. It blinds a person to the reality of a particular situation. The preconceptions of a mindset create assumptions that can lead to failure.

If you want to avoid your mindset biasing the outcome of your decisions, you need to approach every situation with an open mind.

> John 1:46: *"And Nathanael said unto him, Can there any good thing come out of Nazareth? Philip saith unto him, Come and see."*

When Nathanael heard about Jesus of Nazareth, his mindset predisposed him to a prejudicial point of view about people from this city. He thought nothing good could come out of Nazareth. But the situation proved him wrong, because Jesus came from Nazareth and he was perfect.

When you are making decisions, avoid operating on your default position – your mindset. Be open-minded in your approach. Let the situation itself reveal the way it should be handled, rather than jumping to conclusions based on your preconceived views.

(For further study, see: Romans 12:2, Ephesians 4:23, John 8:32, Philippians 2:5, 1 Corinthians 2:16)

12. Lack of foresight

Foresight is the ability to see into the future and make the necessary preparations for it today.

A man of foresight will not take decisions based only on the prevailing situation of today, but gazes into the future to assess what he thinks will happen.

Such decisions, if the foresight is correct, will be able to withstand the test of time because the man has taken account of the fact that time changes things.

In Matthew 25:1-10, ten virgins went out to meet the bridegroom. Five of them took into consideration the possibility that the arrival of the bridegroom would be delayed, so they decided to take extra oil for their lamp. But the other five did not consider the possibility of a delay and so went with the exact amount of oil their lamp would need if everything went to schedule. But the bridegroom was late, and the five virgins that lacked foresight lacked enough oil to keep their lamps lit.

A decision based purely on the present situation cannot withstand the test of time.

In your decisions, consider the changing factors of life.

(For further study, see: Proverbs 22:3, 29:18, Romans 8:28, Luke 14:28, 1 Corinthians 2:9-10)

13. Lack of originality

Originality is the ability to think independently without being influenced by external forces that could cause hindrances.

Someone who chooses to be original will not copy other people's ideas that may contaminate his plan.

Many good ideas die because foreign and unrelated ideas are incorporated from other sources.

It is true that you can learn from other people or plans, but you must not import ideas into your plan without being sure of their reliability and compatibility.

You must make decisions based on the uniqueness of your situation.

Avoid trying to be like somebody else. Avoid making decisions based on what is happening in other people's lives. What works for other people may not work for you.

In Exodus 25:9, Israel was commanded to make a tabernacle according to the instructions God revealed to Moses – not according to the people's own experience or preferences. God emphasized originality. Your decision is likely to be right if you make it according to the reality of your situation and not according to what worked somewhere else. Be original.

(For further study, see: John 8:32, Isaiah 2:3, 30:21, 1 Corinthians 2:9, 2 Corinthians 3:17).

14. Procrastination

Ecclesiastes 3:1: *"To every thing there is a season, and a time to every purpose under the heaven…"*

This verse indicates that there is a right time for decision-making.

A good decision made at the wrong time, whether too early or too late, is likely to end in failure or require adjustments. Many decisions fail because of bad timing, particularly procrastination, which puts off decisions until it may be too late. You can keep postponing and delaying action until the right time passes. Some decisions require immediate attention, but procrastination can make you give excuses that will prevent you from acting at the right time.

If you don't want your decisions to fail, act urgently. Due to the uncertainties of life, you can only be sure of the present time.

(For further study, see: Ephesians 5:15-17, Proverbs 20:4, 27:1, James 4:17, Luke 9:59-62).

15. Overburden

There are some decisions that are too big and complicated to be taken by an individual. Such decisions require the combination of knowledge, intelligence and insight from different people.

When decisions that are supposed to be made by a group are taken by a single person, the potential for failure increases.

Due to the complexity of such decisions, if one person handles it all, their mind may become overcrowded and clouded. This may attract a series of errors due to stress of the mind. A mind that carries more than it is able of carrying will malfunction.

In Numbers 11:11-17, when Moses complained to God that he was overburdened by the care he gave to the Israelites, God gave him seventy helpers to share the burden of the ministry with him. This enabled Moses to share the decision-making tasks with people and so improve the quality of such decisions. If you want to make good decisions you may need to have a team of helpers to work with you in decision-making. Do not do it all by yourself.

(For further study, see: Deuteronomy 1:12, Proverbs 12:25, Luke 21:34, Matthew 11:28, Nehemiah 4:17)

16. Wrong combination

Many decisions necessitate a combination of different materials and people with a diversity of attributes.

If the wrong combination of people or/and materials is selected, it is almost certainly going to jeopardise a good outcome. It is therefore important to choose wisely.

For example, in Judges 7:1-10, Gideon was going to war with 32,000 fighters. However, God told Gideon to send those who were afraid home, and he was left with just 10,000. But it was the right decision. If you wage a war with unwilling people, defeat is almost certain. One rotten potato can infect other healthy ones. Therefore, start a decision-making task with people who are committed to your objectives, not with those who may spoil it, even if that means reducing your team.

The God put the 10,000 remaining soldiers through a test, which only 300 passed. So Gideon was left with just 300 men to fight alongside him. But again, God knew what he was doing. He had found a fault with the other soldiers that Gideon could not see.

Many decisions fail because the wrong people are involved. If you unwittingly select the wrong set of people to work with you, defeat is imminent.

(For further study, see: Exodus 12:38, Numbers 11:4, Matthew 13:30, 22:10, Luke 3:17).

17. Unrealistic ambition

Many decisions fail because the person concerned fails to be realistic in his plans. By merely looking at certain proposals, it will be clear that they are over-ambitious.

A common reason for failure is that some people cannot discern between what is achievable and what is a pipe dream. While it is right to exercise faith in God, it is also right not to test God by having ridiculous expectations. Only be unrealistic in human terms when God has specifically told you to take a step of faith above and beyond what seems possible.

In Luke 14:28-31, Jesus taught that it is not wise to start a project without first counting the cost. Starting a project when you know that you have no resources is setting yourself up for failure.

It is no use just saying, "God will provide", as if God is a slot machine who has to provide everything you want. If you have not specifically heard from God that he will provide for a particular need, you will only bring dishonour to God's name when the project fails. God has promised to supply all our needs, but we must discover what those needs are (what we see as a need may not be what God sees as our need) before claiming the supply.

Similarly Jesus said, in the same Bible verses, that it is not wise to wage war against an enemy you know can't defeat. It is like committing suicide!

It is true that God can lead you to win an impossible battle, no matter what the odds, but never fight such a battle if God has not promised He will fight for you. It is true that God can help you achieve a goal, but never embark on a goal that is unrealistic unless God has promised you success.

Similarly, some people have failed in little things but still believe that they can succeed in bigger things of the same sort. Sometimes our failures are a way of God guiding us to change direction, rather than to persist with wrong objectives for us.

Jeremiah 12:5 states that it is impossible to outrun a horse if you cannot outrun a human being. It's pointless trying. Therefore, before you attempt to conquer big things, wait until you have conquered the smaller things.

(For further study, see: Habakkuk 2:5, Psalm 49:11, Proverbs 24:10, 1 Corinthians 9:24-27, 1 Corinthians 3:11)

18. Inflexibility

Decisions can fail if the person taking it is very rigid and unwilling to change his strongly-held beliefs, even when it is clear that his methods will not work. Such people are unreasonably obstinate.

The person may not be humble enough to accept that his method is not going to fit into his plan. It is possible that this method has worked for the person before but in a new situation or new time, it may not be relevant anymore. It is a wise thing to be open to the possibility of change. Be willing to learn from others. Be willing to bend when you are introduced to better options.

James 3:17 states that one of the characteristics of heavenly wisdom is that it is easily entreated. That is, it can be persuaded. It can change its position when it is necessary. Even when a wise man has made up his mind on an issue, he is ready to change if there is a better idea. Flexibility will make you adaptable to diverse situations.

(For further study, see: 1 Corinthians 9:19-23, 1 Corinthians 10:33, Philippians 4:11-13, Luke 5:4-5, Romans 11:14)

19. Wrong counselling

Who you listen to during your decision-making could influence the outcome of your decision. If you listen to wrong advice from people around you and incorporate this into your decisions, failure may become unavoidable.

It is not wise to take advice on board from a person who has no record of success in the topic you are deciding upon. Or if you do, it should only be after a thorough examination of the advice. Many good visions have collapsed because of bad counsel. Be careful of those you listen to when taking decisions.

In 2 Samuel 13:1-5, Amnon wanted to sleep with his sister, Tamar, and he took counsel from his friend Jonadab. Jonadab did not rebuke him but gave him devious advice on how to achieve his evil plan. Amnon succeeded in raping Tamar, but later lost his life due to the revenge of Absalom – the direct brother of Tamar.

Who is your counsellor? To succeed in decision-making will require that you only get a wise and good counsellor involved. It is not everybody that can advise you. Do not take advice from fools or they will make you foolish. Ensure that every advice is biblical, otherwise reject it.

(For further study, see: 1 Kings 12:6-11, Proverbs 13:20, 14:7, Psalm 1:1, Ephesians 5:6-7)

20. Impatience

Patience is a virtue. It prevents rash decision-making.

Patience will help you to wait for all the relevant details necessary to make a good decision. It will also help you to wait for the best opportunity to implement your decision. Some decisions are too delicate to be made urgently.

In 2 Samuel 5:4-5, David became king over Israel many years after he had been anointed king. He patiently waited for the right time. He endured all the troubles from King Saul.

David must have taken the decision to wait for God's timing, because he had a series of previous opportunities to kill King Saul and take the throne. Instead, David let God clear the way for his reign. Conversely, in 1 Samuel 13:8-10, King Saul was impatient. He chose to make a sacrifice instead of Samuel, because he ran out of patience in waiting for Samuel. His decision contributed to his removal as king of Israel. Impatience will lure you into making a premature decision.

(For further study, see: Romans 8:24-30, James 5:7, Hebrews 11:13-16, Habakkuk 2:3, Genesis 29:20-28)

21. Guilt

Guilt is a feeling of unhappiness originating from the belief that you have committed a sin, or made a mistake that has hurt someone else.

People sometimes make decisions under the influence of guilt, in hope of correcting a mistake they think they have made or to appease their conscience for a sin they have committed.

In such a situation, their decision arises from a guilty heart and self-condemnation. If we are Christians, guilt and condemnation is from the devil. God does not condemn us but convicts us of our sin, so that we can be repentant and forgiven. All that is from the motive of love, as He wants to restore us. That love may include disciplining us, with the aim of bringing us to repentance, but it is never punishment (Romans 2:4).

Every action orchestrated by God is motivated by love not condemnation, for there is now "no condemnation to them which are in Christ Jesus" (Romans 8:1).

Decisions motivated by guilt are rarely long-lasting. In Exodus 9:27-34, the Pharaoh agreed to let Israel leave Egypt. But his action was motivated by a feeling that he had sinned. He acted under the emotion of guilt, but very soon changed his mind. His decision was not motivated by love. Love breeds genuine repentance that causes a permanent change of action.

If your decision is motivated by guilt in the hope of making up for a sin or mistake, it will only be a matter of time before your emotion vanishes away and you find yourself regretting your decision. Guilt generates a chain of regrets that never ends.

If you take a decision under guilt or regret, you are under the control of negative emotions. Only under repentance will you make a decision that lasts and that you don't regret.

In Numbers 14:40-45, Israel chose to enter into the land they once rejected. Their decision was motivated by guilt, not love towards God. Therefore, there was no permanent repentance. Shortly after this incident, they angered God again due to their consistent disobedience.

A decision motivated by guilt usually fails because it comes with misrepresentation – it does not show your real self. It is a consequence of negative emotion, not love. Do not make a decision in the hope of releasing yourself from guilt – only repentance and asking forgiveness can achieve that. Instead, let your decisions be based on genuine need.

(For further study, see: Psalm 103:12, Romans 8:1, Hebrews 8:12, Jeremiah 31:34, 50:20)

22. Bitterness

Bitterness originates from an unforgiving spirit. Decisions made under bitterness can never be right. This is because you are not likely to give proper regard in your decision to the person you hold bitterness against, even if they could play a vital role in such decisions.

A man under the control of bitterness will be blinded, unable to appreciate those who can help his decision succeed because he hates them.

Bitterness hinders good reasoning. It will not let you reason rightly, especially if the decision relates to those you are bitter towards.

In 1 Kings 22:8, the king of Israel would not seek prophecy and guidance from the prophet Micaiah because he hated him. Even if the prophet had the right guidance, the king would ignore it. Hatred will not let you bring the right people into your decisions.

Similarly, in Genesis 37:8, Joseph's brothers made the decision to sell him into slavery because they hated him. They later regretted their action, after many years. It is only a matter of time before a decision made under the control of bitterness will unravel.

You will need to check your heart and motivation. Ask yourself what makes you take certain decisions and what makes you avoid certain people in your decision-making.

(For further study, see: Ephesians 4:31-32, Hebrews 12:14-15, Proverbs 10:12, Romans 12:17-21, Ecclesiastes 7:9)

23. Following the crowd

Sometimes decisions are made because of general popular opinion. Unfortunately, experience has proved that the majority is not always right. If your decision is based on popular views, you may be in for a big surprise.

In Numbers 13:32, after Israel had sent spies into the land of Canaan, they came back and the majority of them warned Israel that the people of Canaan were too strong to defeat. The people of Israel chose not to trust God that they could overcome the Canaanites, believing instead the majority of the spies. As a result, the Israelites had to stay in the desert for 40 years, and the spies were proved wrong when a new generation of Israel successfully invaded Canaan.

Do not follow popular opinion unless you have proved it to be right and in accordance with the Bible.

(For further study, see: James 4:4, Proverbs 5:20-21, Psalm 118:8-9, Matthew 16:16, 2 Timothy 4:3).

24. Lack of purpose

Purpose is the reason behind an action. It is the reason why you want to take a decision and the justification for it.

Purpose helps you to identify what to achieve and the expected results.

Where the purpose is not clear, there will be a lack of direction. Many decisions fail because the reasons for them are not clearly established.

Therefore, before you take any decision, identify the purpose behind it. Explore within yourself the objectives you want to achieve through such decisions.

Ephesians 1:11 states that God works all things out according to the counsel of His will. This implies that every decision and act of God is to achieve His pre-planned agenda. In every single one of His actions, God has a particular aim in mind. This gives Him direction in whatever He does.

Similarly, in John 5:30, Jesus clearly stated the rationale behind His decisions. Everything he did was designed to carry out the will of the Father, who sent Him into this world. This is the reason why every decision Jesus took was right. When the purpose for an action is established ahead of the action, there will be direction and fulfilment.

(For further study, see: Daniel 1:8, Exodus 9:16, Ecclesiastes 3:1, Acts 17:11, Isaiah 49:4).

25. Lack of commitment

Commitment brings dedication to a cause or plan. It makes you devoted and means you are prepared to give everything to your cause. Commitment solidifies your heart towards the cause and makes you do whatever you can to achieve the plan. Decisions that will yield the desired fruits will require commitment, both at the planning and execution stages.

In order to make quality decisions, you may need to spend your vital resources in gathering relevant information. Unless you are committed, the cost of decisions may discourage you. Many projects fall below the desired standard because the person in charge decided not to pay the price necessary to achieve the desired quality.

In 1 Kings 22:5, in order to make the best decision about going to war, Jehoshaphat and the king of Israel made a series of consultations with prophets for divine guidance. This shows their commitment to their decision-making. Sometimes, you may need to travel a long way or pay a high price to gather vital information to aid your decision-making. You will only be able to pay such a price if you are committed to your decision. At times, you may need to make personal sacrifices in order to make a quality decision. A committed heart is ready to pay the price.

(For further study, see: 2 Corinthians 6:4, Luke 9:62, Colossians 3:23, 2 Timothy 4:7, Philippians 3:13)

26. Non-acknowledgement of God

> Proverbs 3:6: *"In all thy ways acknowledge him, and he shall direct thy paths."*

Many decisions fail because God is set aside in the process. Your decision will end up in disaster if you fail to acknowledge God in the process.

To acknowledge God means to bring God into the whole decision and let Him direct the course of events. At times, due to deception, some people believe that they can handle certain situations by themselves and they don't see any reason why they should bring God into the matter. They will soon discover their folly.

In Joshua 9:1-15, Joshua and the elders of Israel decided to enter into a covenant with the Gibeonites – without consulting God. They later discovered that they had acted under deception. Unfortunately, it was too late to change the agreement because it was made under an irrevocable oath. When you bring God into your decision-making, He will shed His light into all the details to enable you to see the hidden factors that could be very important.

(For further study, see: 1 Samuel 30:8, Psalm 32:8, Jeremiah 10:23, Jeremiah 9:23, Psalm 37:5)

27. The courage factor

Courage gives us the ability to take difficult decisions and some decisions fail because of a lack of courage. With courage, you will be able to make decisions irrespective of the danger and challenges involved. Timidity, anxiety, fear or cowardice will prevent you from facing certain challenges involved in your decisions.

In Numbers 13:29-33, Caleb was so courageous that he was ready to wage war against the inhabitants of the Promised Land, even though some of them were giants. Courage made him believe, despite the strength of the opposition. But the fearful and cowards focus only on the strength of the opposition, while neglecting their own advantages. The Israelites forgot they had God on their side.

Lack of courage will hinder you from seeing how you can overcome the challenges. It required courage to take the decision to walk on water, as Peter did in Matthew 14:29. It also required courage for David to face Goliath in battle despite his lack of experience. In 1 Samuel 17, David chose to fight Goliath irrespective of the possibility of defeat. That is courage. You will need courage to take decisions that expose you to serious danger and possible destruction.

(For further study, see: Daniel 3:16-17, Joshua 1:6, 10:25, Psalm 31:24, Philippians 1:28)

28. Slothfulness

This is a lazy unwillingness to work. A slothful person is always reluctant to commit himself to any activity that will require work on his part. When a slothful person makes a decision, he avoids any scenario that requires him to put in some effort. He will always seek the easy way out, or the easy way to do something, so as to avoid commitment.

Such a person prefers to shift the hardest responsibilities onto other people, and always has excuses for inactivity. He will give excuses for making decisions that are poor quality and involve little commitment. His slothful habit will make him blind to a better way of achieving his plan, because he wants to avoid all the challenging routes.

In Matthew 25:14-30, Jesus told the story of a man who gave talents to his servants according to their ability and then went on a journey. This man did not instruct his servants what they should do with the talents he gave them. He probably wanted them to use their initiative to make their own decision about what to do with the talents. Who they were would determine the decisions they would make about the talents. On his return, the master discovered that the servant who was slothful did nothing with his talent.

This slothful servant gave a series of excuses to justify his lazy approach to the talents he received from his master. In Matthew 25:26, the master refers to this servant as wicked and slothful. Such a man will always prefer to do nothing while others are busy. Therefore, if you want to make a good decision, you must be prepared to put the hard work in when it is needed. Don't take a decision with the intention of avoiding commitment and energy.

(For further study, see: Proverbs 18:9, 24:30-31, 26:13, Ecclesiastes 10:18, Hebrews 6:12)

29. Drunkenness

A person who is 'drunk' is someone who is overcome by an excessive intake of alcohol.

Anyone who is under the influence of alcohol is not in a sound state of mind for decision-making. Alcohol impairs our ability to reason and act well.

People can also be overcome by excessive anger, anxiety, joy or sorrow, all of which has a similar result. These emotions cloud their thinking, robbing them of the ability to make good decisions, because they lose control of their mind and become irrational and illogical.

In Genesis 9:21-23, Noah got drunk on wine and took off his clothes in his tent. The alcohol made him lose his normal inhibitions and this had a negative impact on those around him. His ability to reason accurately was seriously impaired.

Also, in Matthew 14:6-7, Herod was 'drunk' with pleasure and made an unwise offer to Herodias's daughter. He did not think deeply about his promise to her. Either the joy of celebration or sheer lust took over his mind and he made a stupid decision. The result was the death of John the Baptist.

In Matthew 26:69-75, Peter was 'drunk' with fear and he denied Jesus. Fear of men took over him and he could not think properly before denying Jesus.

Furthermore, in Daniel 4:30, King Nebuchadnezzar got 'drunk' on his own achievement and he sinned against God. His success took over his reasoning. Finally, in Genesis 4:3-8, Cain was so 'drunk' with jealousy that he slayed his brother, Abel. A spirit of jealousy completely took over his reasoning, so that he did not think properly about the implications of his impending action. You are drunk when you have lost your mind and are incapable of thinking straight. In this situation, you become vulnerable and prone to wrong decisions.

Therefore, avoid making important decisions when you are not in a sound mind – for whatever reason.

(For further study, see: Luke 21:34, 1 Corinthians 14:32, 1 Peter 1:13, Proverbs 16:23, 1 Thessalonians 5:6-8)

30. Fantasy

This is the act of dwelling on sweet but impossible thoughts. Fantasies can lure us into making a series of lofty assumptions that result in failure. Fantasies are by definition unrealistic, but their attractiveness can seduce our imagination and lead us astray.

Someone who allows a fantasy to encroach on his real world will operate on untested and unproven theories or ideas that usually breed disaster. He will just assume that things will turn out well, despite making none of the required effort.

It is good to imagine things, but what is imagined must be in agreement with the Word of God. Every imagination that is contrary to the Word leads to self-delusion. Decisions based on futile fantasies without any basis in reality will end in failure.

In 1 Samuel 17:39, David refused the armour of King Saul because he had not tested it out before. He wasn't used to fighting in cumbersome armour. He did not assume that the armour would work for him simply because it worked for King Saul. A man deluded by fantasy believes that anything will work for him.

In Joshua 8, Joshua planned the invasion of the city of Ai despite the fact that God had already told him that the city was his. He still realised that success would not come easy – he and the people had to play their part. But a man of fantasy believes that success will come whether he makes the necessary plans or not.

If you want to make quality decisions, don't operate on assumptions but on certainty.

(For further study, see: Deuteronomy 29:19, Revelation 3:17, Proverbs 30:12, 14:12, 2 Corinthians 10:5)

31. Greed

Greed is an unregulated, unchecked desire to have more than what you have and often more than what you are entitled to. A decision made by a greedy person is usually one that is based on selfish gains. A greedy person will not consider the interests of other people involved, but only consider himself. Such decisions can cause bitterness and pain.

In 2 Kings 5:20-27, a decision made by Gehazi was motivated by greed. It resulted in his destruction. He chose to take for himself the gifts his master had refused. Whenever you are making decisions, ensure that selfish gain is not your motivation.

In 1 Kings 21:1-16, King Ahab requested the vineyard of Naboth because of sheer greed. When Naboth refused his request, he conspired with his wife to organise the death of Naboth. Their plot to murder Naboth succeeded, but a curse was brought upon their home. When greed takes over the heart of a man, he thinks selfishly – ignoring other people's wishes or needs.

Your decision will not be right if you act under the motivation of greed, because selfishness is always at the expense of other people.

(For further study, see: Ecclesiastes 5:10, Luke 12:15, Proverbs 15:27, 28:22, 1 Timothy 6:6-10)

32. Pleasures

A pleasure is simply something that you enjoy, particularly luxurious things, but you have to be careful with pleasures. They can be dangerous and addictive, and often drag people into worldliness.

Someone taken over by the love of pleasure is likely to hate anything that could bring pain or involve sacrifice. For example, hard work can be difficult and painful even though it is normally beneficial – and even if the rewards may not be seen for a long time. A person given to pleasure will always avoid decisions that could bring pain, so he will not be ready to compromise comfort – irrespective of future gains or rewards. A person given to pleasure is not ready to pay the price of a quality decision. He will prefer to have fun when he supposed to be working hard to make a good decision.

Luke15:12-25 tells the story of a prodigal son who took his inheritance and chose to go to a far country where he was free to spend his inheritance on a life of pleasure. His love for pleasure badly influenced his decision on how to handle his inheritance. A person given to pleasure will likely make a decision that will waste his wealth and talent, due to the attractions of pleasure.

If you want to make quality decisions that won't waste your limited resources, get rid of love for pleasure. When you work hard to achieve your dream, you will be able to eat the good fruits of your labour in good time. Delay pleasure and discipline yourself to make good decisions, irrespective of the price involved.

(For further study, see: Proverbs 21:17, Luke 8:14, Ecclesiastes 7:4, Isaiah 47:8-9, 1 Timothy 5:6)

33. Envy

Envy makes a man unhappy about the achievement of another person. The decision of an envious person will be influenced by the achievement of his neighbour. He will be running the race of another man. You are likely to make wrong decisions if you are motivated by envy, so before you finalise a decision, check out what is motivating you.

If you pursue the plan of another person, which is beyond your capability, failure is inevitable. Ecclesiastes 4:4 states that other people's success generates envy in us. Envy is a negative emotion that influences its victims to act wrongly.

In Genesis 4, Cain wished that he had won God's approval like his brother Abel had. So because he was jealous of his brother's achievement, he became angry and took the evil decision to kill his brother.

If you want to make good decisions in life, you must avoid focusing on the good things going on in the life of your neighbour. Be original, both in thought and action. Do not chase the dream that you see your neighbour chasing, because you may not have the same resources as your neighbour, and the dream may not be what is good for you.

(For further study, see: James 3:16, Exodus 20:17, Song of Solomon 8:6, Hebrews 13:5, Proverbs 6:34)

34. A rebellious spirit

Rebellion is an act of resistance to an authority. A person suffering from the activity of a rebellious spirit is likely to make wrong decisions under certain situations, because he or she will not submit to authority.

Such people are likely to be always finding faults in those who have authority over them. A rebellious person's decisions will frustrate or infuriate an established authority, almost certainly generating friction, controversy and conflict. And such decisions can also have an effect 'up the chain of command', negatively impacting those who are in authority.

If your decisions frequently cause the disapproval of those above you, it might be because you have a spirit of rebellion, but not always, as there are bullies in every walk of life, who abuse their power, or it may simply be that you are not doing your job well. But if your decisions are constantly aimed at pulling those above you down, it is very likely that you are suffering from a rebellious spirit.

1 Samuel 15:23 tells us that King Saul's decision to disobey God was due to his rebellion. His actions were influenced by a spirit of rebellion. The spirit interpreted the situation to him and made him see a justification for operating in disobedience. If you are always looking for a reason to disobey authority, it is likely that you are suffering from a rebellious spirit.

(For further study, see: Proverbs 17:11, Hebrews 3:15, Isaiah 14:12-25, 63:10, Numbers 16:1-3).

35. Prayerlessness

Prayer is communication with God. It also involves seeking God's approval concerning a situation.

In 1 Samuel 30:7-8, David didn't rush into a decision without discerning God's will. He took the time to enquire of God as to whether he should chase after the band of raiders who had taken his family captive. God gave David His assurance that he would recover his family and all his possessions, so David set off and rescued everyone who had been taken.

In some other situations when people requested God's approval, instead of God giving a direct answer, He gave wisdom so that people could make their own decisions correctly. In 1 Kings 3, King Solomon requested wisdom from God and it was granted to him. This enabled Solomon to make good decisions during his reign as king, and he became renowned throughout the world.

For you to make a wise decision, you will need to pray to the God of wisdom to give you wisdom. A lack of prayer can open the door to demonic manipulation of a decision, ruining what otherwise would have been a good decision. Without prayer, demonic spirits can find an open door and a free hand to operate against your purposes. So pray before, during and after decision-making.

(For further study, see: Psalm 14:2, Isaiah 43:22, Jeremiah 5:3, 10:21, Ezekiel 22:30-31)

36. Stubbornness

A stubborn person does not change his attitude or position on something. He is determined to do whatever he decides to do. He does not tolerate counsel or a better opinion that could make him change his position or mind or course of action. The heart of such person is hardened as regards his action.

Before King Pharaoh finally allowed Israel departed from Egypt, in Exodus 13:15, he had refused their freedom in many times. He was thoroughly stubborn. He chose to be stubborn despite not knowing the full consequences of his actions. A stubborn person will refuse to bend and change his decision, even though he doesn't know what the result of that stubbornness will be.

If you want to make a good decision, respect superior and contrary opinions, otherwise, you may face serious negative consequences for your stubbornness. In Numbers 14:39-45, Moses advised Israel not to invade the land of the Amalekites and Canaanites but they stubbornly pursued their plan. They failed and lost the battle. A stubborn person is wise in his own eyes. He does not listen to any opposing opinion that may make him change his position on an issue.

(For further study, see: Psalm 106:15, Proverbs 1:24-31, 29:1, Romans 2:5, Jeremiah 5:3)

37. Evil unity

Evil unity is when you enjoy the cooperation of a team, but in a wrong direction. It is when people team up with you to do the wrong thing. It is similar to what sociologists call 'the herd instinct' – where people go along with what everyone else is doing, without thinking for themselves, or peer pressure where everyone feels pressurised to fit in with a group and not question decisions. Unity is a good thing, but not when it is abused in this way.

The crowd will not always support you when you are right. Sometimes you have to go against the flow. Alternatively, when you are wrong, selfish people might support you in your decision because they have something to gain out of it, or ignorant people might support you because they lack understanding of the issue.

Therefore, don't rejoice just because you are enjoying the cooperation of other people; only rejoice if you know that unity is taking you in a good direction.

In Genesis 11:1-4, the people of the earth came together to build a tower to reach heaven. It was an evil unity, joining together for the wrong reasons. God eventually came down to confuse their languages and frustrate their plan. The human plan failed because somebody equated unity with a right decision. The two do not always go together.

In Numbers 14:1-35, the whole congregation of Israel united to protest against God, and brought destruction on themselves. This clearly shows that not every cooperation among people is good, and you can't assume your decision is right just because you have the support of your team, church, family or friends.

Some people agree with you for selfish reasons, others because they don't know any better, some just because they don't want conflict, and some because they are too afraid to share their own opinion.

Irrespective of the level of cooperation from people, thoroughly test your decision to ensure that it is right in the eyes of the Lord.

(For further study, see: Proverbs 11:21, 1:10-11, Exodus 23:2, Numbers 16:2, 1 Samuel 15:9)

38. A lying spirit

A decision could be wrong because the person has suffered the attack of a lying spirit. This is a spirit from hell that deceives people into taking wrong decisions.

In John 8:44, Satan is described as a liar and the father of all lies. He is a spirit and through his demons of lies, he can deceive a person to act wrongly. Therefore, it is important that you subject your decision to a series of tests and verification before implementation.

People who seek a quick gain or want to 'make a fast buck' usually fall into the trap of a lying spirit. Similarly, greed, impatience and unregulated ambition will expose you to the attack of a lying spirit.

When a person is under the influence of a lying spirit, all his decisions will look good and achievable. The victim of a lying spirit will not see that he is under the influence of this spirit.

Ideas that appear too good to be true could be ideas from the lying spirit. Walking in the flesh opens the door for the entrance of lying spirits.

(For further study, see: Hosea 11:12, 1 Kings 13:18, 22:19-23, Acts 5:3, Zephaniah 3:13)

39. An idolatrous spirit

This is an ungodly attachment to anything that takes the place of God in your life. Whatever has become your idol will control your heart and make it difficult for you to hear the voice of the Spirit of God, so that you cannot be guided into the truth.

Whatever controls your heart will control your decisions and your spiritual sensitivity.

In Joshua 7, Achan stole riches from the plunder that was supposed to be set aside for God's use. His love for these valuables either stopped him remembering that God had warned the people not to do such a thing, or they enticed him to ignore that warning.

If you want to take right decisions in the sight of God, you will need to keep your heart dedicated to Him above all. Never let idols replace Him in your affections, or they will control your heart and your decisions.

If you give your heart to money, you will not be able to hear God when He is giving you an instruction regarding finance. If you put your job before everything else, you will not be able to hear God when He wants to guide your career.

King Solomon gave his heart to many women and he forgot the counsel of God regarding marrying foreign women. Their influence turned his heart away from the Lord, persuading him to build temples to false gods, and it destroyed his legacy (1 Kings 11:1-13).

To be able to hear God very clearly in your decision-making, you need to get rid of idols in your life. In Genesis 19:26, the wife of Lot looked back and became a pillar of salt. She probably looked back to Sodom because of her strong attachment to her possessions in the city that was being destroyed by God's judgement. Perhaps materialism was her idol.

(For further study, see: Deuteronomy 7:4, 30:17, Jonah 2:8, 1 Corinthians 10:14, 1 Samuel 15:23)

40. Desperation

Desperation is a condition of panic that breeds hopelessness. A desperate person is likely to be reckless in his effort to get out of a situation that makes him afraid.

The consequences of desperation can include distraction, anxiety, worry, pain and rashness. A desperate person is not likely to think well before taking decisions. He acts under the grip of hopelessness and he is too much in a hurry to get out of the situation to make a good decision.

In 1 Samuel 28:6-7 King Saul, driven by hopelessness into desperation for a revelation from God about the future, took the decision to seek help from a diviner or medium instead.

When God seems to delay to intervene in our affairs, we can become desperate for a solution, and turn in the wrong direction for help. A decision driven by hopelessness will lead us down the wrong path.

In Exodus 14, Israel became desperate for deliverance when they saw Pharaoh pursuing them. In their desperation, they started acting like unbelievers, insulting their spiritual leader, Moses. If you allow desperation to overwhelm you, it may lead you to do wrong things.

To make a quality decision, you will need the peace of God to rule your heart. But if you do become desperate, use that desperation to drive you to seek God, not to give up or do something wrong.

(For further study, see: Philippians 4:6, Jeremiah 17:7-8, Psalms 55:22, 142:6, Deuteronomy 31:8)

41. Wilful ignorance

This is a situation where someone intentionally makes himself unaware of relevant information. Information is available, but the person chooses to ignore it.

You will be committing wilful ignorance if you intentionally choose to ignore relevant facts that could help you make a right decision, or fail to look for that information when you know that it can be found.

For example, an atheist commits wilful ignorance if he or she knows that plenty of good books and arguments for Christianity are available, but refuses to bother looking at them. Perhaps he/she prefers to be an atheist and doesn't want to look at opposing arguments and evidence in case they undermine the atheist's confidence in his/her beliefs.

Many people make wrong decisions today not because the information that could help them is not available, but because they are too lazy or impatient to seek out that information.

In Hosea 4:6, God said that because Israel rejected knowledge, He would reject them. Knowledge was available but they wilfully rejected it and thereby made a series of avoidable wrong decisions.

So before you make decisions, explore every possible avenue that could aid your decision-making. Seek appropriate information and approach a relevant counsellor that could help you.

(For further study, see: Leviticus 5:17, James 4:17, Luke 12:48, Job 21:14, Hebrews 2:3)

42. Spiritual insensitivity

This is the inability to perceive spiritual influences around you, and a lack of awareness of spiritual messages and presences.

Decisions could be wrong not because God has not given guidance but because the person did not sense it. Equally, a decision could be wrong because the person failed to recognise demonic involvement.

Some people are dull of hearing in a spiritual sense, such that they are not able to receive divine revelation to guide them in their decision-making.

Even when God speaks to such people through fellow human beings, His Word or His arrangement of circumstances, they are unable to perceive it. Lack of spiritual sensitivity also hinders the ability to discern between good and evil.

God wants to guide you into making right decisions but you need to have listening ears.

Job 33:14 says that God can speak more than once to people yet they don't perceive it. The consequence of not recognising God's guidance is following the wrong direction. It is a big loss to miss divine guidance for decision-making.

2 Timothy 3:7 confirms that some people are always learning plenty of things but are never able to understand the truth about God, and so will live in error. If you don't want that to be you, you will need to improve your spiritual sensitivity. You can do this by a closer walk with God, regularly reading and planting the Word of God inside your spirit.

(For further study, see: Isaiah 6:9, Ezekiel 12:2, Hebrews 5:11, 1 Corinthians 2:14, Romans 8:5-8)

43. A seducing spirit

This is a spirit that manipulates people into taking decisions they would not have taken naturally, and acting in wrong ways. This spirit operates through temptation. It has a charming power. It can make wrong things appear attractive to a person in order to lure them into sin or mistakes.

In Genesis 3, in order for Satan to seduce Adam and Eve into disobedience, he highlighted the attractions of the forbidden fruit. Adam and Eve then took a decision under demonic seduction and acted in error. They had not planned to disobey God – Satan exploited their weakness.

Equally, you may not intend to disobey God or make a wrong decision, but you can be deceived and lured into it. Satan can make everything look good and promising, before you realise what he has done. Naturally, without such a seductive influence, you would not make a wrong decision, but Satan is cunning and clever. That is why it is important for you to be careful when you suddenly find yourself under pressure to act in a particular way. It could be the influence of the spirit of seduction, trying to pressurise you to act against your best intentions.

Similarly, when every bit of your plan looks so promising and faultless you may need to re-evaluate it. It may be too good to be true! If you are not having problems, that is suspicious, because the enemy tries to disrupt good things. If everything is going smoothly, it may be because the enemy has no reason to oppose something that is going his way.

The spirit of seduction may be presenting you with fake promises to lure you into a false sense of security, which leads to a decision you will soon regret.

Every excitement that rises up within you during decision-making must be tested, to ensure that it is not the spirit of seduction trying to plant fake hope in you and motivating you to act in error.

(For further study, see: 1 Timothy 4:1, Ezekiel 13:10, Mark 13:22, 1 John 2:26, Revelation 2:20)

44. A delay in asking for help

Some decisions have the potential to be fruitful but if you delay asking for the necessary help it could bring disaster.

Some people will not ask for help because of personality problems. They may distrust other people, or their ego may be too strong and lead them to think they don't need help. Others may feel demeaned and weak if they have to ask for help. Or of course, it may simply be that some people do not recognise that they need help, or are too late to see it.

You need to understand when you need help and be able to ask for it from the right people. In your decision-making, when you get to the end of your wisdom and no longer know what to do, you should recognise that it is time to seek help from God and other people.

It is foolish to keep on going when you have no idea of the right direction. The wise thing to do is to ask for help. Do not wait until the situation gets out of control before you cry for help because by then, it may be too late.

In Matthew 14:30, Peter cried to Jesus when he started sinking. If he had delayed, he would have sunk below the water. There is a right time to ask for help.

In 2 Kings 4:1, a widow cried to Elisha for help because the creditor was coming to take her two sons away. If she had hesitated to approach Elisha for help, she might have lost her two sons. In your decision-making, when you no longer know what to do next, seek help.

In Exodus 18:14-20, Moses failed to ask for help from the elders of Israel. He was judging the whole nation on his own – too big a task for just one man. His father-in-law counselled him to seek assistance from the elders, and Moses heeded his advice. You must be able to acknowledge when you need help, otherwise, you will mess up your decision.

(For further study, see: Exodus 17:12, 1 Chronicles 12:22, 1 Kings 12:6-8, Proverbs 15:22, 20:18)

45. Communication problems

A decision could come under threat due to a communication problem between people involved in the decision. When the facts and figures related to a decision are misunderstood or misinterpreted, errors could arise that could threaten the success of the decision.

It is therefore necessary to ensure that all the parties involved in the decision-making are at the same level of understanding. All the parties should have the same exposure to the information necessary to make a good decision.

In Genesis 2:16-17, God told Adam and Eve not to eat the forbidden fruit in the garden. But in Genesis 3:3, Eve misquoted the statement God gave them. She added that God told them not to touch the forbidden fruit, as well as not to eat it. This kind of misinterpretation, misquotation and incorrect information could hinder effective decision-making, especially when more than one person is involved.

For effective decision-making, every fact and figure must be applied as stipulated by the source, and communicated to others effectively. In Genesis 17:1, God visited and spoke to Abraham but the presence of his wife, Sarah, is not mentioned. In many places in the Bible, it is recorded how God spoke to Abraham without Sarah being there. This implies that Sarah did not have access to the same divine revelation as Abraham. She undoubtedly had to rely on second-hand information through her husband, so when it came to joint decision-making for the two of them, Sarah would not have been at the same level of understanding as Abraham, which may have hindered their agreements and decision-making, perhaps contributing to Sarah's bad decision to tell Abraham to have a child by Hagar (Genesis 16).

To avoid complication in decision-making and implementation, it is necessary that every party involved has the same access to relevant information.

(For further study, see: Psalm 56:5, 2 Peter 3:16, John 2:19-21, 11:12-13, 21:23)

46. An untrained mind

A mind which has been trained in the knowledge of the decision to be taken will perform well. Your ability to reason well and make right decisions about an issue will be enhanced by the knowledge you have about the topic of the decision.

For example, you may not be able to take right decisions about marriage when you don't have the right and required knowledge about it. Therefore, before you take any decision, educate yourself about the necessary knowledge.

In Numbers 13, Israel chose some of their men to be spies, to gather relevant knowledge about the land of Canaan before the invasion. The knowledge gained should have empowered them in their decisions about invading Canaan. In fact, it had the opposite effect because of their fear of the giants in the land, but they should have used the knowledge to make a successful invasion instead of allowing it to put them off.

Many decisions fail because the person taking the decision has little or no knowledge about the issue being considered. To empower your mind to make the correct conclusions about a particular topic, you will have to feed your mind with the right information.

(For further study, see: Colossians 3:10, Ephesians 4:23, Romans 12:2, Mark 2:22, Hebrews 10:22)

47. Lack of order

Decisions can fail because of a poor arrangement of events. If things are not done in the right order, then a decision could be more complicated than it needs to be, or even go in the wrong direction.

For example, if what should be put first was placed last, the outcome of the decision could be significantly different. In Genesis 1 and 2, before God created human beings, He ensured that everything necessary for our survival already existed. People would have died of thirst or hunger if He had not first created water and food. Therefore, it is important for you to know how events are connected and related to each other when making decisions. Explore the sequence of events necessary to achieve your desired objective, and as your decision is implemented, monitor what is done to see that the right progression of events takes place, as they are interconnected and dependent on each other, otherwise, you might not achieve the right outcome.

(For further study, see: Genesis 1:26, 1 Timothy 2:13, 1 Corinthians 14:33, 14:40, 15:45-49)

48. Ignorance of the Word of God

Not knowing what the Bible says and being unaware of the promises of God concerning certain situations can lead to unbiblical approaches/solutions that bring failure.

Before you make any decisions, you will need to see if there are specific instructions from the Bible about the issue involved. If not, there will always be a relevant principle, so you need to identify that. Similarly, before you can make right decisions, equip yourself with the promises of God concerning the matter. A lack of biblical guidance will lead to blunders in decision-making.

For example, before you make a decision about who to marry, get biblical guidance on marriage. If you want to do business with another person, get biblical advice about such alliances. 2 Timothy 3:16 says: "All scripture is given by inspiration of God, and is profitable for doctrine, for reproof, for correction, for instruction in righteousness..."

Hebrews 10:7 indicates that Jesus lived his life according to the written Word of God. All his decisions were dictated by that. This is the secret of wise decisions.

(For further study, see: John 5:30, 6:38, Psalms 19:7-8, 119:105, Matthew 22:29)

49. Lack of self-motivation

Self-motivation is when a person strengthens himself by finding good reasons to achieve a purpose, irrespective of the challenges. It is likely to be needed when there is nobody else around to offer such encouragement. And it is definitely needed when other people are discouraging, so that you do not lose your determination to forge ahead with your decisions.

It is difficult for a discouraged heart to produce good decisions. Self-motivation will always be required to some degree when making decisions, especially when people around you seem to be negative towards what you are doing.

In 1 Samuel 30:6, David had to motivate himself when everybody around him became negative towards him due to their losses. Under these distressing circumstances, David still needed to make decisions about recovery which he had to get right. So David chose to motivate himself by remembering the goodness of God in his life and spending time with God.

Similarly, in 1 Samuel 17:33-37, David had to motivate himself when King Saul was trying to discourage him from fighting Goliath. Saul gave David good reasons why he thought David would not be able to fight Goliath, but David gave his own good reasons why he thought he could defeat Goliath.

When people around you become negative towards you during decision-making, you will need to motivate yourself. If you give in to demotivation from people, you may well get your decisions wrong.

(For further study, see: Job 13:15, 19:25, Psalm 27:1, Jeremiah 20:11, Habakkuk 3:17-18)

50. Character deficiency

In many situations, your decisions reveal who you are. Faults in your character could create faults in your decisions.

For example, when a person who is unloving makes decisions that affect fellow human beings, there could be a lack of consideration for human comfort in such decisions. A wicked man is likely to make wicked decisions. A reckless person is likely to make reckless decisions.

Such decisions can sometimes cause a revolt among the affected people, and sooner or later, bad decisions will be overturned. Mark 7:21 reveals that the heart of a man gives birth to his thoughts and actions. Your heart determines your character, which will determine your decisions.

In Matthew 2:16, King Herod decided to slay all the children in Bethlehem under the age of two because he was deceived by the wise men. Only a person with a wicked heart would make such a decision. Therefore, before taking certain decisions, check the nature of your heart and weigh your character. Many decisions fail because a faulty heart produces faulty decisions.

(For further study, see: Proverbs 27:19, 28:12, 28:28, Ecclesiastes 9:3, 10:5)

51. A spirit of error

Our decisions can fail if we act unknowingly under the influence of the spirit of error. The spirit of error is a spirit that blinds the mind of people to the truth, so that they unknowingly act under error.

It is not likely that somebody will intentionally make mistakes – people come under the attack of the spirit of error without realising it. Such victims will operate without having access to the truth that could have improved their decisions.

In 1 Samuel 13:13, Samuel rebuked King Saul for behaving foolishly by performing the role meant for the priest. Saul acted in error. He tried to justify his error, but that did not prevent him from being punished for it.

Furthermore, in 2 Samuel 6:6, Uzzah died because he touched the Ark of the Covenant. He didn't intend to be irreverent, but his decision caused his death. He would not have taken such a decision if he knew he was doing wrong. The spirit of error prevents a person from accessing the truth.

In Leviticus 10:1-2, Nadab and Abihu, the sons of Aaron, died because they erroneously offered unauthorised fire to the Lord. They did not follow God's instructions for this kind of sacrifice, so they were punished for their disobedience. They were isolated from the truth during their decision-making.

It is therefore important for you to ensure that you have all the necessary facts and figures before making your decisions. During decision-making, you must also be aware of false doctrines that could lead you into error. Do not apply principles and doctrines you are not sure of when making decisions.

(For further study, see: 1 John 4:4-6, 1 Corinthians 2:12, 2 Timothy 4:3, Colossians 2:8, 2:23)

52. Deficiency in spiritual warfare

Decisions can fail because of a lack of knowledge about spiritual warfare. Every good decision will face opposition from different sources. It is therefore important for you to understand certain forces that may arise against your decision, both at the planning stage and execution stage.

Spiritual warfare is called 'warfare' for a good reason. It is deadly serious – and can be as dangerous as waging a physical war against enemies, so it is vital that we don't overlook this aspect of our spiritual life when making decisions.

There are at least five major forces that could arise against your decision, to frustrate it, and you should be ready to contend with them as they attempt to hinder and destroy your good decisions – whether at the planning stage or during execution.

1. The devil

Ephesians 6:12 states that our major enemy in life is the devil and all his demons: *"For we wrestle not against flesh and blood, but against principalities, against powers, against the rulers of the darkness of this world, against spiritual wickedness in high places."* This applies as much to our decision-making as every other aspect of life.

In his attempt to frustrate your good decisions, he may send his demonic forces into operation to attack your mind or raise human agents against you. According to Ephesians 6:16, the devil may fire his flaming arrows against you. This; he does by attacking your mind with a series of wrong thoughts and ideas that could derail you or confuse your mind.

James 4:7 advises that we should resist the devil whenever he comes to attack our mind or bring opposition in our lives. To resist means to refuse to yield to his demonic influence and suggestions.

2. The flesh

The flesh – our human weaknesses – is another enemy that could hinder your good decision-making.

> 1 Corinthians 9:25-27: *"And every man that striveth for the mastery is temperate in all things. Now they do it to obtain a corruptible crown; but we an incorruptible. I therefore so run, not as uncertainly; so fight I, not as one that beateth the air: But I keep under my body, and bring it into subjection: lest that by any means, when I have preached to others, I myself should be a castaway."*

These verses show that your flesh could become your stumbling block in decision-making. Your carnal desires could speak wrong things into your mind. Your body could become tired when you are supposed to pray against the forces of darkness. Your flesh could demand pleasures when you need to be self-controlled. It is your responsibility to keep your flesh under your control, otherwise, it will influence you to make wrong decisions.

3. Human enemies

Other people who oppose you can be a hindrance to good decision-making.

> Psalm 59:2-3: *"Deliver me from the workers of iniquity, and save me from bloody men. For, lo, they lie in wait for my soul: the mighty are gathered against me; not for my transgression, nor for my sin, O LORD."*

In this psalm, David prayed to God against the human enemies that rose against him. Also, Nehemiah 4 reveals how certain men rose against the decision of Nehemiah to rebuild the walls of Jerusalem. Nehemiah and his team had many struggles against people who wanted to frustrate their project. You should be ready to resist any human being who wants to frustrate your decision, directly or indirectly – though not using violence, of course, except in self-defence.

4. The world

The world and its human systems, whether political, cultural or social, could become the enemy of your good decisions.

> John 16:33: *"These things I have spoken unto you, that in me ye might have peace. In the world ye shall have tribulation: but be of good cheer; I have overcome the world."*

In this verse, Jesus was preparing the minds of His disciples for trouble from the society around them. Sometimes, your decisions may be contrary to the world system, and if you are not courageous enough, you might be tempted to cave in to pressures from the world.

Your decisions may bring you into serious conflict with popular views and beliefs, or the traditions and culture of the world in which you live. Unless you are courageous, you may change your decisions because you don't want to appear like an outcast in the eyes of the world.

5. The fear of death

The last enemy that you may need to fight against in your decision-making is the fear of death.

> 1 Corinthians 15:26: *"The last enemy that shall be destroyed is death."*

> Hebrews 2:14-15: *"Forasmuch then as the children are partakers of flesh and blood, he also himself likewise took part of the same; that through death he might destroy him that had the power of death, that is, the devil; and deliver them who through fear of death were all their lifetime subject to bondage."*

These verses indicate that the fear of death has put many people under bondage. If you are afraid of death, you may not be able to take certain decisions because of the level of risk involved. Therefore you will need to assure yourself that Jesus has conquered death for you and you can't die until God is ready to take you home.

Ephesians 6:18 advises that you must be alert all the time. That is, be watchful, because the enemy may arise against you at any time and from the least expected source. Always engage in spiritual warfare through prayer, in order to preserve your decisions. Don't forget to pray and walk in faith.

(For further study, see: 2 Corinthians 10:4-6, 1 Corinthians 16:13, 1 Timothy 1:18-19, Galatians 5:17, Hebrews 11:33-37)

53. Acting under a curse

A person placed under a curse will be influenced by a demon that supervises the curse, controlling the person's thinking process when it comes to decisions related to that curse.

For example, if a woman was cursed to never have children, every decision she makes in the area of fertility will be controlled by the demon in charge of the curse. As a result, every decision the woman makes will only serve to advance infertility in her life. Even if she wants to marry, she will decide to marry someone who will not fulfil her wish for a child.

Until the curse is broken and the demon supervising the curse cast out of her life, she will always make decisions that promote barrenness in her life.

2 Samuel 15:31: *"And one told David, saying, Ahithophel is among the conspirators with Absalom. And David said, O LORD, I pray thee, turn the counsel of Ahithophel into foolishness."*

In this verse, David prayed that God would cause Ahithophel's advice to Absalom to be foolish. This was a curse. The Lord answered the prayer of David and spiritual forces started orchestrating the events in Ahithophel's life needed to fulfil David's request.

2 Samuel 17:14: *"And Absalom and all the men of Israel said, The counsel of Hushai the Archite is better than the counsel of Ahithophel. For the LORD had appointed to defeat the good counsel of Ahithophel, to the intent that the LORD might bring evil upon Absalom."*

This verse shows that the people around Ahithophel lost respect for his opinion. The spirit supervising the curse on Ahithophel was influencing both the people and situations around him in order to bring to pass the prayer of David.

2 Samuel 17:23: *"And when Ahithophel saw that his counsel was not followed, he saddled his ass, and arose, and gat him home to his house, to his city, and put his household in order, and hanged himself, and died, and was buried in the sepulchre of his father."*

This story tells what Ahithophel decided to do when he found that his counsel was being ignored. He took the decision to kill himself. Someone of a sound mind does not normally commit suicide, so it is clear that the spirit that invaded his life due to the curse was controlling his thinking process and how he felt about the situation in his life.

When a man is under a curse the spirit that supervises the curse will be exercising control over his thoughts and perverting his view of the situation around him to produce the desired result of the curse.

Mark 5:1-5: *"And they came over unto the other side of the sea, into the country of the Gadarenes. And when he was come out of the ship, immediately there met him out of the tombs a man*

> *with an unclean spirit, who had his dwelling among the tombs; and no man could bind him, no, not with chains: because that he had been often bound with fetters and chains, and the chains had been plucked asunder by him, and the fetters broken in pieces: neither could any man tame him. And always, night and day, he was in the mountains, and in the tombs, crying, and cutting himself with stones."*

This story tells of a mad man who was cutting himself with stones. Naturally, he would not cut himself if he was in his right mind, but because he was under the influence of stronger demonic forces, he was not aware of the wounds he was inflicting on himself, or he was unable to stop himself.

When someone is making decisions under demonic control, those decisions will destroy him, but often; the person is unaware of the demonic scheme until the damage is beyond repair. For example, addiction is demonic, although, some people are more easily influenced into addiction because they have a physical or psychological weakness that demons exploit. A man under the captivity of the spirit of addiction will not see his wrongdoing, or not be able to admit it, and neither will he be able to resist the demonic urge rising inside him. This is why the first step to defeating addiction is to admit that you have a problem!

> Mark 5:15-17: *"And they come to Jesus, and see him that was possessed with the devil, and had the legion, sitting, and clothed, and in his right mind: and they were afraid. And they that saw it told them how it befell to him that was possessed with the devil, and also concerning the swine. And they began to pray him to depart out of their coasts."*

The people of this region asked Jesus to leave. They were under the influence of demonic forces that ruled over the region. When a man is under demonic influence, he will make the decision to run away from the place of deliverance, or to hate the vessel of deliverance that could set him free from demonic captivity. The demon supervising the affliction will gain control of his thinking process, to force him to always avoid the place where he could experience deliverance.

When such a person is invited into a church where he is likely to find freedom from hidden yokes in his life, the demon supervising the affliction will control his mind to avoid visiting such a gathering. The man under this demonic influence will always have a good reason for avoiding good churches. So we must remember that it is the demon supervising his affliction that is speaking through him, not himself, when our invitation is rejected.

Not every thought that comes up in our heart comes from the Holy Spirit. Sometimes, demonic spirits put thoughts into our mind. This is the reason why it is essential to bring every step in decision-making before God in prayer. Let God get involved in your decision-making and ensure that you maintain sound spiritual activities in your life as you make your decisions. It is also important that you submit yourself to Christian mentoring to help you maintain your spiritual discipline, particularly when in the process of making big decisions.

(For further study, see: Proverbs 26:2, Proverbs 6:27, Ecclesiastes 10:8, Haggai 1:6-11, Mark 5:1-5)

54. Wrong spiritual combination

A decision could go wrong if people with a negative spirit form part of your team. When you work with people who have a contrary spirit to your spirit, this could set in motion events that will frustrate your decision. For example, if one of your team turns into your enemy as a result of having a contrary spirit, it will be difficult or impossible to work together. If someone hates you or disagrees with your methods, they will fight your plans and undermine you. There will be a negative spiritual atmosphere which will hinder decision-making.

Amos 3:3: *"Can two walk together, except they be agreed?"*

To succeed with another person requires agreement both in the physical and spiritual realm. You must be of the same spirit regarding decisions, otherwise, you will create a negative spiritual combination. For example, how can you pray with your enemy and expect the prayer to be answered? It is impossible. Heaven does not work with disunity. Therefore, before you collaborate with anybody in your decision-making, ensure that the person is not your enemy or evil-wisher.

(For further study, see: Acts 15:38-40, Exodus 17:12, Genesis 11:6, 1 Chronicles 12:33, Matthew 18:19)

55. Emulation

This is the act of imitating or copying what other people do or have done. It is not always bad to emulate people, but you must know what you are emulating. If you want to act as other people are acting but you lack their experience, grace and gifting, there could be problems. Decisions may fail if you ignorantly and unwittingly copy other people's methods or projects.

If you desire to be like other people, you will need to ask yourself if you have their attributes – the attributes that make them succeed. In Acts 19:14-16, the seven sons of Sceva wanted to emulate Paul but because they lacked Paul's anointing and gifting, they failed shamefully. They ended up in defeat instead of victory.

You can incorporate what you have seen working in other people into your decision-making, but you must ensure that you are able to manage that effectively. But you must remember that just because something works for somebody else does not mean it will work for you.

In 1 Samuel 8:4-22, Israel asked Samuel for a king because they wanted to be like other nations. Their motive and decision were born out of emulation of other nations around them. Unfortunately, their request was not in total agreement with God's plan for them, but they insisted. Psalm 106:15 states that though God gave the Israelites what they wanted when they were wandering in the desert with Moses, God sent "leanness into their soul", or as most newer translations put it, "a wasting disease" (NIV/RSV/AMP) or "plague" (NLT). Decisions originating from emulation can bring unimaginable negative consequences.

(For further study, see: Exodus 23:2, Deuteronomy 12:30, 2 Kings 17:15, Matthew 23:3, Proverbs 1:10-11)

56. Not counting the cost

You can make wrong decisions if you fail to take into proper consideration the price to be paid. It is important to understand the price tags of our decisions. Even good decisions have a cost attached, and without proper costing, it will be like working in ignorance in your decision-making.

In Luke 14:28, Jesus advised that we should do proper costing before starting a project. This will enable you to foresee the challenges ahead before they surface. Decisions often go wrong because someone fails to look into every necessary detail that increases the price tag. If you want to make a good decision, you need to get all your cost analysis right. Understand the provisions required and how much they will cost. History is littered with unfinished projects and half-completed buildings due to lack of funds and materials. This often happens because of a lack of proper planning and costing.

(For further study, see: Proverbs 19:2, 2:11, 13:16, 18:15, 24:27)

57. Poor foundation

The foundation determines the future of the building built upon it. The building could be made of good materials but because of its poor foundation, it will have a short life span. Decisions that will yield long-term positive results must have a solid foundation, otherwise, there will soon be calamity.

When a decision faces the test of the time, it is the strength of its foundation that determines its longevity. Decisions based on shallow thought and unverified statistics will not be able to survive attacks that demand in-depth knowledge and certainty.

The ultimate foundation for every decision is God. If your decision is based on total assurance that God is behind it, when challenges come, you will triumph with your decision. If your decision is based on doubt, when challenges come, your faith will falter.

If your decision has no solid source of resources to fund it, when there is a serious financial need to move the decision forward, you will be unable to make progress, and the whole project may be at risk. Therefore, to avoid disastrous decisions, you must establish a solid foundation that will be unshakable during trial and opposition. For a decision to pass the test of time, there must be enough resources to sustain it. Make sure you have a credible level of knowledge about the resources needed to make a success of your decision.

> Luke 6:49: *"But he that heareth, and doeth not, is like a man that without a foundation built an house upon the earth; against which the stream did beat vehemently, and immediately it fell; and the ruin of that house was great."*

Jesus told His disciples that it is not wise to build a house on a poor foundation because when the storm and wind come against the house, it will fall – an expensive loss. Therefore, you can avoid or reduce calamity if your decision is based on a solid foundation that can sustain it, both during the planning and execution stages. The foundation must include sustainability of the decision at every phase of its implementation.

(For further study, see: Galatians 6:3, James 4:13-14, Job 27:18, 1 Corinthians 3:12-15, 8:2)

58. Lack of focus

Focus or concentration is essential to good decision-making, as it allows the minimum application of energy for the maximum return. Without consistent focus, you can waste lots of time and energy for little result.

Where there is strong focus, there is attention to every necessary detail. With focus; you will be able to give your best to your cause.

Lack of focus makes a person easily swayed from the right path. If you lose concentration, you could miss vital facts and figures that are essential to the success of your decision. There will also be weak willpower. Without focus, little challenges will overcome you. You will not be able to apply yourself well to decision-making in the absence of good concentration.

> *Matthew 6:24: "No man can serve two masters: for either he will hate the one, and love the other; or else he will hold to the one, and despise the other. Ye cannot serve God and mammon."*

Jesus told His disciples that it is impossible to maintain allegiance to two masters at the same time. You cannot give equal loyalty and concentration to two different avenues. There will be a lack of focus on one if you are focused on the other. Therefore, if you don't want to produce a poor decision, you will need to give your maximum concentration and loyalty to that decision.

(For further study, see: Proverbs 4:25, Ecclesiastes 9:10, Hebrews 2:1, Colossians 3:23-24, Luke 9:62)

59. Inadequate anointing

The anointing of the Holy Spirit is an enabler. He enables Christians to function beyond their natural ability.

> *1 John 2:27: "But the anointing which ye have received of him abideth in you, and ye need not that any man teach you: but as the same anointing teacheth you of all things, and is truth, and is no lie, and even as it hath taught you, ye shall abide in him."*

This verse reveals that anointing is a teacher. The quality of your decisions will depend on the level of teaching and counsel you receive from the Holy Spirit. The more infilling of the Holy Spirit you have, the greater will be His influence upon your life. This implies that you are likely to make decisions of low quality if you are not full of the Holy Spirit. Conversely, a Christian who is filled with the Holy Spirit is likely to make wise decisions because he receives guidance and counselling from the Spirit who lives within him.

The more you yield yourself to the prompting of the Holy Spirit, the more you will enjoy His influence over your life. Therefore, you need to have a long-term plan of how to build a good relationship with the Holy Spirit so that He can have a greater influence on your decisions.

(For further study, see: Acts 2:4, 4:31, 13:52, John 14:26, Isaiah 11:2)

60. Weak will-power

Will-power is the strength of your will to carry out your decision or action. The strength of your will-power determines the level of your tenacity when you face hindrances. A strong will-power enables you to refuse to quit due to frustration. So if you have a weak will-power, a little opposition can feel like a serious set-back and make you abandon your plan. It is impossible to triumph over frustration if you don't have the will-power to succeed.

A man of weak will-power gives a series of excuses to justify his failure or inaction. In 2 Kings 2:1-15, Elisha pursued Elijah with the aim of getting a double portion of the anointing that was upon Elijah. Along the journey, Elisha was exposed to a series of challenges that were capable of stopping him from following Elijah, but Elisha's strong will-power sustained him.

Elisha probably considered a double portion of Elijah's anointing as necessary for him to succeed in his ministry. He might have concluded that if he didn't obtain the double anointing he wold give up his ministry. You will be able to exhibit strong will-power over certain decisions if you see no alternative to success in such decisions.

(For further study, see: 2 Timothy 1:6-7, Ephesians 3:16, 6:10, 1 Corinthians 16:13, 2 Corinthians 12:9-10)

61. A modelling problem

A model is a preliminary work of construction; built to help produce the final product, usually on a much smaller scale than the final building or buildings. It is generally believed that if a model is perfectly made, it will give a perfect guide to help create the final product. If the modelling is wrong, then the project resulting from it may well turn out wrong. And if there is no model at all, then the final product may be completed with a serious lack of necessary details, or fail to fulfil the aims of the project.

> Exodus 25:9: *"According to all that I shew thee, after the pattern of the tabernacle, and the pattern of all the instruments thereof, even so shall ye make it."*

In this verse, God showed Moses a model of the tabernacle He wanted him to build. This model would guide Moses in producing an accurate tabernacle.

Plans can seriously go wrong if there is no model to give a guide or if there is something wrong with the model used. Therefore, before you start making a decision or implementing one, see if there is an already existing model to work from or if a model can be made.

> Hebrews 12:1: *"Wherefore seeing we also are compassed about with so great a cloud of witnesses, let us lay aside every weight, and the sin which doth so easily beset us, and let us run with patience the race that is set before us."*

This verse tells us that there are many witnesses around us who we can use as role models or examples to guide our decision-making. There are many Bible characters that you can study to see how they made decisions. Similarly, there are many people around you whose decision-making you can learn from. Study the lifestyles and work methods of people who have made decisions similar to the one you are about to make and use their insight to improve your decision-making.

(For further study, see: Hebrews 8:5, Exodus 39:42-43, 1 Chronicles 28:11-12, Ezekiel 43:10-11, 1 Peter 3:6)

62. Wisdom factor

Wisdom is the application of knowledge. Usually before a decision is implemented, it is in theoretical form or conceived in the heart.

When it is time to implement a decision, wisdom will be required to apply those ideas and turn them into reality. An inability to accurately translate an idea from its theoretical form into practical form is evidence of a lack of wisdom. Decisions may fail if we are unwise in the way we apply concepts and theories in the real world.

> Exodus 35:30-32: *"And Moses said unto the children of Israel, See, the LORD hath called by name Bezaleel the son of Uri, the son of Hur, of the tribe of Judah; and he hath filled him with the spirit of God, in wisdom, in understanding, and in knowledge, and in all manner of workmanship; and to devise curious works, to work in gold, and in silver, and in brass."*

Here; Moses had received knowledge, revealed by God, about building a tabernacle for the Lord, but he lacked the technical knowledge and skills to translate all the ideas God gave him into reality. So the Lord sent people with the construction and artistic abilities needed to work with Moses and help him to translate the plans into a tangible form.

If you have a good idea but you don't know how to make it happen, seek the help of wise and experienced people, otherwise, you will probably mess things up. It is one thing to have an idea; it is quite another thing to be able to implement it. A lack of the wisdom required can damage any good idea.

(For further study, see: Proverbs 4:7, 14:1, 24:3,6, Jeremiah 10:12)

63. Pride

Pride is an excessively high opinion of oneself. A proud man believes in himself and thinks he is greater than he actually is. It is an overestimation of personal qualities.

Pride gives false security to its victim. It can make you feel secure in yourself, even when danger is around you and you have no reason to feel secure. A proud man relies only on his own ideas and knowledge. Such a person finds it hard to learn from fellow human beings, even though their knowledge will help him. A proud man prefers to fail rather than have to seek help. To him, asking for help is evidence of inferiority and weakness. Unfortunately, the decisions of such people often fail because they reach the end of their own wisdom and their plans can't work without the help of others.

> James 4:6: *"But he giveth more grace. Wherefore he saith, God resisteth the proud, but giveth grace unto the humble."*

This verse teaches us that God will not support the plans of a proud man; He will not give him the enabling grace that would help his purposes succeed. It implies that the decision of a proud man is doomed to failure.

> Proverbs 16:18: *"Pride goeth before destruction, and an haughty spirit before a fall."*

This verse states that pride leads to destruction. So if you see pride in someone, it only a matter of time before you will see them fail. A proud man will not ask for directions, though he does not know the way ahead. A pride man will not listen to wise counsel, even if it will aid his decision. Your decision may fail if you are prone to pride. Humble yourself and take advantage of the many useful resources around you and the advice of others that can help advance your decision.

(For further study, see: Proverbs 13:10, Romans 12:3, Luke 18:9-14, Revelation 3:17, Ezekiel 28:17)

64. Hard work factor

No decision succeeds without some degree of effort and endurance. Behind every great decision is hard work. Laziness prevents us from putting in the necessary effort to achieve our objectives.

> James 2:26: *"For as the body without the spirit is dead, so faith without works is dead also."*

No matter how great an idea appears to be, without hard work, it will not materialise. Faith on its own is not profitable if it is not supported with corresponding actions. Decisions will fail if not backed up with the practical application required.

Proverbs 21:25: *"The desire of the slothful killeth him; for his hands refuse to labour."*

A lazy man folds his hands and his desires fail to materialise. Some people's plans never get further than the preparatory stage because to enter into the implementation stage requires more effort than they are willing to put in. Laziness is a recipe for failure.

Proverbs 24:30-31: *"I went by the field of the slothful, and by the vineyard of the man void of understanding; and, lo, it was all grown over with thorns, and nettles had covered the face thereof, and the stone wall thereof was broken down."*

These verses indicate that without hard work, a place that is supposed to produce good fruit will end up producing weeds and thorns. If you take time to plant your vineyard but fail to apply the effort and time to dress and maintain the vineyard in a good state, then it will end in ruin and loss.

Proverbs 12:24: *"The hand of the diligent shall bear rule: but the slothful shall be under tribute."*

The New Living Translation puts this teaching in this succinct way: *"Work hard and become a leader; be lazy and become a slave."* If you want to become a leader in your field or get to the top in your profession, it won't happen while you sit idly by and wait for it. High achievers are always hard workers, as well as smart workers. If you want to see your good plans yielding success, step up to the plate when the need for hard work comes.

Proverbs 14:23: *"In all labour there is profit: but the talk of the lips tendeth only to penury."*

A modern way of putting this verse would be: *'A lazy person is 'all talk and no action'."* Hard work is required in every stage of a good decision if the expected ends are to be achieved. If you know you are lazy, make the effort to change your behaviour or you will regret it.

(For further study, see: Proverbs 6:10-23, 12:11,24, 14:23, 2 Timothy 2:6)

65. The liberty factor

A decision can fail if you have to rely on other people to complete it or to implement it. Sometimes, implementation requires permission from another person or people, and if the permission suffers a delay or places unhelpful conditions on the implementation, it may threaten the success of the whole project.

You will need a certain level of liberty for you to be able to carry out decisions as you wish. Similarly, some decisions involve agreement from many people and if those people are not genuine in their involvement, or cannot agree for other reasons, it may well affect the decision under consideration.

> Luke 22:25-26: *"And he said unto them, The kings of the Gentiles exercise lordship over them; and they that exercise authority upon them are called benefactors. But ye shall not be so: but he that is greatest among you, let him be as the younger; and he that is chief, as he that doth serve."*

Jesus here teaches that in this world, the kings and leaders in charge have great power over their people, but Christians are not to be dictatorial but servants of other people. Some kings and leaders offer help to their subordinates to succeed in their endeavours, and so call themselves benefactors, but because they have the power to set the rules, often their subordinates' plans will have to change at the whim of the leaders, otherwise, they will not get any help at all.

This implies that though you may have good plans and ideas, those with the power or money to help you implement your plans will have the last say on what happens and that may affect the outcome of your plans. Therefore, if you want to stay in control of your project so that it will be realised in the way you want it to be, you need to limit your dependency on other people. You are not in control of your plans until you are in control of your decisions. In many situations, benefactors have stolen good ideas from their subordinates and made them their own. In other cases, benefactors have frustrated good plans by refusing to give the help needed at a crucial stage.

(For further study, see: John 5:7, Acts 3:2, 2 Corinthians 3:5, Psalm 146:3, 118:8-9)

66. The consistency factor

Consistency is an act of regularity while inconsistency is an act of irregularity. This could be in terms of methods, approach, dedication or interest. Without a consistent approach, the outcome will become unpredictable and there will be a lot of uncertainties. Inconsistency will build a cloud of doubt around your decision.

A decision could fail because there is no consistency in the manner of handling the situations that affect the decision. For example, if your mood towards your decision is always fluctuating, this may well delay or change your decision. A good mood will enable you to give your best to your plans, but a bad mood will negatively affect your handling of the situation.

Fluctuation in the support you receive could also hold up the progress of your decision. Similarly, a consistent supply of resources is essential if a decision is to succeed without delay.

> Hebrews 10:23: *"Let us hold fast the profession of our faith without wavering; (for he is faithful that promised;)..."*

This verse admonishes us to be consistent in faith. If your faith dwindles as regards your decision, you will waver in your commitment to it, which may bring disaster to the final outcome.

> James 1:6-8: *"But let him ask in faith, nothing wavering. For he that wavereth is like a wave of the sea driven with the wind and tossed. For let not that man think that he shall receive any thing of the Lord. A double minded man is unstable in all his ways."*

This verse shows that an inconsistent man is not trustworthy and therefore, heaven will not give him support. Furthermore, people are going to be slow to render you support when they notice your inconsistent approach to your plan. Consistency can win you support both from man and God but wavering will rob you of vital support. Inconsistency will make you lose track of events that could be vital to the success of your decision.

(For further study, see: Numbers 14:24, 1 Thessalonians 5:21, Psalm 18:21-22, Colossians 3:23-24, Luke 9:62).

67. The temperament factor

Temperament describes an individual character or disposition in terms of reaction to situations. It determines your emotional stability and how you respond to circumstances and people, especially unforeseen or unexpected challenges.

If you lose your temper quickly, your reaction to a situation may be hasty and unwise. Your temperament will always become an issue when you have to make an urgent decision. A person of bad temperament may fail when it comes to making an urgent decision, because pressure proves whether you can stay under control or whether you lose it. Similarly, your ability to maintain a good and acceptable character under challenging situations may be determined by your temperament. Bad temperament is the root cause of emotional instability.

> 1 Corinthians 9:27: *"But I keep under my body, and bring it into subjection: lest that by any means, when I have preached to others, I myself should be a castaway."*

This verse reveals the conscious effort needed to keep our temperament under control. If you don't rule over your emotions, they will rule over you. Unregulated emotion can destroy any good idea, especially when it comes across sudden and unexpected obstacles.

In Genesis 34, Dinah the daughter of Jacob was sexually violated by Shechem and when Jacob's sons Levi and Simeon became aware of this, they slaughtered Shechem and all the men of his city. Their temperament ruled over them and dictated their reaction to such an unexpected incident. People of bad temperament often react without considering the consequences of their actions. Jacob said to Simeon and Levi: *"Ye have troubled me to make me to stink among the inhabitants of the land, among the Canaanites and the Perizzites: and I being few in number, they shall gather themselves together against me, and slay me; and I shall be destroyed, I and my house"* (verse 30).

Your decision may fail because of your unrestrained reaction to sudden and unforeseen circumstances. You will need to train yourself to keep your cool, irrespective of the challenges that you may face. (For further study, see: Proverbs 25:28, 16:32, 14:17, 29:11, Ephesians 4:26-27)

68. The negative attitude factor

Your attitude can have a serious impact on your decision-making. Negativity in yourself breeds negativity in others, undermines confidence, breeds dissent and, most importantly, damages your faith.

For example, whenever a person of negative attitude faces a difficult situation, he will say it is impossible to defeat the opposition, or nobody can solve the problem, or things are terribly bad and there is no way forward, or the only solution is to quit, or it will be a waste of time to press forward, etc.

Such a negative attitude closes the door to possibilities that could help you succeed. If you are always negative when you face unforeseen difficulties, your decision is likely to fail. And if you have a negative attitude, people that could help you succeed will be repelled and walk away from you.

> Numbers 13:31-32: *"But the men that went up with him said, We be not able to go up against the people; for they are stronger than we. And they brought up an evil report of the land which they had searched unto the children of Israel, saying, The land, through which we have gone to search it, is a land that eateth up the inhabitants thereof; and all the people that we saw in it are men of a great stature."*

In this story, most of the men who went to spy out the land had a negative attitude when they became afraid of the inhabitants of the Promised Land. They came back thinking that it was impossible to take the land. They said their enemies were too strong. As a result of their negative attitude, they lost sight of their advantages and the strength they had to overcome their enemies. They even forgot that they had God on their side, who had been fighting their battles for them.

A negative attitude will form a veil over your understanding, such that you will not be able to identify your advantages in a particular situation.

(For further study, see: 1 Samuel 16:7, Ephesians 4:26, Philippians 2:5, Job 13:15, Colossians 4:2)

69. Thoughts factor

> Proverbs 23:7: *"For as he thinketh in his heart, so is he: Eat and drink, saith he to thee; but his heart is not with thee."*

This verse indicates that your thoughts create your world, and the outcome of your decision is determined by the kind of world you have created around yourself.

This is because the kind of thoughts you develop in your heart determines your character, and your character will determine your attitude, and your attitude will determine your words and actions, which in turn create many of the circumstances of your life. Your life will attract what you think about continuously – whether negatively or positively.

If you think your decision will fail, then failure will be attracted to your decision. For your decisions to come out good, you have to think good about them. Good thoughts will create a good imagination and a passion inside you, and generate hope and positive expectations. This will indirectly strengthen your will-power, which will give you the determination to persevere when trouble strikes. With good thoughts you will create a good external environment for your decision to thrive on.

With good thoughts, suddenly resources that were once scarce became abundant, wisdom that you once lacked comes to your mind, helpers that were once scarce get attracted to you. You can't have bad thoughts and expect a good result.

(For further study, see: Philippians 4:8, Proverbs 21:5, 12:5, 24:9, Romans 12:2).

70. The old glory factor

This relates to your past achievements. Old glory, if not carefully controlled, can hinder your performance in decision-making. If you allow your former achievements to dominate your thought, you may create a spirit of pride within you.

Your past achievements can lead you to become arrogant in the way you see yourself, thinking of yourself more highly than you ought to do. Your previous accomplishments may trick you into underestimating the challenges of your present decisions. Furthermore, because you have succeeded in a similar endeavour before, you may think you will definitely succeed in your present endeavour. This deception may make you become careless and unprepared. Many decisions fail because the person involved develops fake expectations as a result of previous successes.

> Joshua 7:2-4: *"And Joshua sent men from Jericho to Ai, which is beside Bethaven, on the east side of Bethel, and spake unto them, saying, Go up and view the country. And the men went up and viewed Ai. And they returned to Joshua, and said unto him, Let not all the people go up; but let about two or three thousand men go up and smite Ai; and make not all the people to labour thither; for they are but few. So there went up thither of the people about three thousand men: and they fled before the men of Ai."*

In this Bible story, Joshua has just defeated the people of Jericho and now they face the people of Ai for battle. Joshua chose very few soldiers to fight against Ai, in the hope that it would be an easy fight. After all, the Israelite army had just defeated the mighty Jericho. Alas, Joshua and all his army were surprised by small Ai, because they underrated them. Old glory can deceive. Your poor preparation for your present challenge may be due to the deception that you have won before so you can always win again.

If you are to always win, you will need to face every new challenge with fresh ideas and planning.

(For further study, see: Matthew 9:16-17, Romans 12:3, Proverbs 26:12, Isaiah 37:21-29, Psalm 127:1-2)

71. Indecision

Hesitation because of indecision can prevent good decisions being made. The inability to make up your mind in time about the direction or option to take could destroy your decisions. If you delay a decision or action, you can miss an opportunity that could advance your decision, and that may never come again.

Your indecision could be due to double-mindedness. If you struggle to make up your mind, you may lose what would have been the good result of your decision. Alternatively, your indecision could be due to fear of the unknown, and in this case, you will need to deal with your doubt before it is too late. Lack of courage in general could also produce indecision. In both cases, you will need to strengthen your inner being and find the courage to move on.

Another reason for indecision may be that you lack the required knowledge to deal with the situation. In this case, you will need to find the knowledge that will empower you to make the right decision.

The doors of opportunity to succeed in your decision may be open to you right now, but if you delay, such doors may close and your decision may suffer for it. Unfortunately, indecision is a decision you have subconsciously made to lose the opportunity to control the affairs of your situation. Whenever you fail to make a decision, you are losing the power to determine the expected result of your situation. The longer you remain indecisive, the greater the chance that you or your situation will suffer as a result.

In Luke 23:13-25, the Jews brought Jesus before Pilate for him to condemn Jesus to death, but Pilate chose to make no decision on the matter. Unfortunately, his lack of a decision was tantamount to a decision to allow Jesus' accusers to do they pleased with Jesus. Pilate's indecisiveness made no difference to the situation in the end, in fact, it precipitated Jesus' crucifixion, because he angered the crowd and was forced to kill Jesus in order to keep the peace. Therefore, your lack of decision or hesitation is unlikely to save your decision from calamity, and may bring that calamity about.

(For further study, see: James 1:6-8, 1 Kings 18:21, Matthew 14:31, John 12:42, Acts 24:25)

72. Negative surprises

A lack of preparation for unforeseen circumstances could destroy your decision. If sudden challenges arise and there is no plan to deal with such negative situations, then a decision could come to destruction. Unexpected opposition could frustrate a good decision.

It is good to hope that everything will go well, just as planned, but it is also good to envisage possible challenges. For your decision to go as planned, there must be a plan to deal with every contingency. Your decision is not yet well planned until you have a plan to deal with unforeseen problems that could arise on the way.

In Matthew 25:1-10, ten virgins went out to meet their bridegroom, but only five of them took into consideration the possibility that something might go wrong. The other five did not prepare for a delay in the groom's arrival, and while waiting for the groom, the oil for their lamps ran out. The five that had prepared for such a situation by bringing extra oil entered the wedding ceremony, but the other five went to fetch more oil, and by the time they came back the door was shut.

The success of your decision could depend on the level of your foresight – how well you are prepared for bad surprises.

(For further study, see: James 4:14, Proverbs 16:9, Ephesians 6:14-16, Ecclesiastes 9:12, 1 Thessalonians 5:6)

73. A wrong belief system

As a Christian, you believe in God and His commandments, but you also have certain personal principles and philosophies that silently control your thoughts and actions. This forms your belief system, which shapes how you view and approach situations.

In principle, there is nothing wrong in having personal opinions on many subjects, but if they are contrary to the infallible Word of God, they could bring disaster to your life. As a human being, you are free to run your own life with your personal principles and philosophies, but you must ensure that they are in agreement with the Word of God. A wrong belief system could destroy or damage your decisions.

> Mark 14:64: *"Ye have heard the blasphemy: what think ye? And they all condemned him to be guilty of death."*

In this verse, the Jewish council chose to execute Jesus because his life and teaching violated their belief system. The Jewish religious leaders interpreted every teaching and good word of Jesus through their erroneous belief system. Their decision was fuelled by their wrong beliefs, which they had constructed into a set of traditions in addition to the Law of Moses.

Unless your belief system originates from the Word of God, it will always lead you into error.

> 2 Corinthians 10:5: *"Casting down imaginations, and every high thing that exalteth itself against the knowledge of God, and bringing into captivity every thought to the obedience of Christ…"*

This verse commands that we should eliminate any imagination and every pretension that is contrary to the written Word of God. This means that any personal belief that runs against God's Word should be discarded.

So, be aware that your decision is likely to go wrong if it is founded on your wrong belief system.

(For further study, see: Isaiah 8:20, Jeremiah 8:8-9, Colossians 2:8, 1 Timothy 6:20-21, 1 Corinthians 2:6)

74. Risk taking

Every decision comes with a level of uncertainty. In many situations, you are not sure what the outcome of your decision will be. You will always find yourself at a corner where you have to take a certain risk. If you delay taking the risk, your decision may suffer, and if you take an unreasonable risk, your decision may also suffer. It is therefore very important that you act wisely when it comes to risk taking. You must be ready to take risks but at the same time, you must minimise the chances of failure as much as you can.

Wisdom will help you avoid unreasonable risks, while faith will help you to take a risk that will advance your decision.

> Ecclesiastes 11:4: *"He that observeth the wind shall not sow; and he that regardeth the clouds shall not reap."*

This verse admonishes you not to wait for the perfect time before you embark on a certain action. If you delay your decision, you may regret it.

In some situations, you have no choice but to take a risk, irrespective of the level of safety. In 2 Kings 7:1-14, four lepers had to make a decision as they faced two uncertain choices. Whichever option they chose would expose them to severe risk, but they went ahead with one of the alternatives and it ended in a miracle. These four lepers identified the fact that they had no choice but to take a risk. Failure to act promptly might have made them lose their lives. In such a situation, only faith in God can help.

> Proverbs 3:5: *"Trust in the LORD with all thine heart; and lean not unto thine own understanding."*

Put your faith in God, so that you can see yourself taking risks to advance your decisions.

(For further study, see: Ecclesiastes 11:1-3, Matthew 14:29, 6:34, Joshua 1:9, Ephesians 5:15-17).

75. Demonic control

Sometimes, people's decisions are dictated by demonic powers. In 1 Samuel 16:14-15, it is recorded that the Spirit of the Lord departed from Saul and demons started to trouble him. In 1 Samuel 18:10-11 and 1 Samuel 19:9-10, Saul repeatedly attempted to kill David with a javelin due to demonic influence. The demons that dwelled inside Saul influenced his decisions, making him try to kill David.

Demonic control still happens today. If someone has been hateful towards you, it may be that the person is under the influence of a demon of hatred. And if you have decided to injure a fellow human being, it possible that you have been manipulated by demonic forces. Similarly, a decision borne out of lustful desire is likely to be under the control of a demon of lust. If you make the decision to take what does not belong to you, you are likely to be under the influence of a demon of covetousness. A decision that glorifies doubt is likely to be under the demon of doubt. A decision to take revenge is likely to come from the demon of unforgiveness.

Therefore, you will need to investigate the spirit that is influencing your decision. Every spirit is known by its fruits. Every ungodly decision is likely to come from an ungodly spirit, and every godly decision is empowered by the Spirit of God.

> Romans 14:17: *"For the kingdom of God is not meat and drink; but righteousness, and peace, and joy in the Holy Ghost."*

This verse indicates that a decision that is of God will not violate the basic principles of the kingdom of God, which are: righteousness, peace and joy in the Holy Spirit.

(For further study, see: 1 Timothy 4:1, 2 Corinthians 4:4, Matthew 12:42-46, Ephesians 2:2, James 4:7)

Seven

DEALING WITH YOUR WRONG DECISIONS

Some years ago, my family wanted to put money into an investment with the help of a friend. We made the decision to invest all our money in this project – emptying our bank account. Before we finally took that decision, we prayed and fasted and waited on God to give us a word to rest on. We believed that we received this word from the Bible:

> Acts 10:11-15: *"And saw heaven opened, and a certain vessel descending unto him, as it had been a great sheet knit at the four corners, and let down to the earth: wherein were all manner of fourfooted beasts of the earth, and wild beasts, and creeping things, and fowls of the air. And there came a voice to him, Rise, Peter; kill, and eat. But Peter said, Not so, Lord; for I have never eaten any thing that is common or unclean. And the voice spake unto him again the second time, What God hath cleansed, that call not thou common."*

In this vision, God told Peter not to call anything impure that God has made clean. In other words, do not refuse what God has allowed you to have. With this Bible verse as our guide, we went ahead with the plan, ignoring everything else that seemed to not be in alignment with the Word of God. The kind of help our friend was giving involved a series of unbiblical matters, but we ignored all these and erroneously quoted the verses from Acts 10.

In the end, the project failed and we lost every cent in our bank account. My wife and I were devastated, because we believed we had a word from God that gave us the assurance that the project was of God. Its failure convinced us that something must have been wrong. There must have been something that we did not see. We dealt with our wrong decision as follows:

1. We sought understanding

We asked God to reveal to us where we got things wrong. Whenever you get a decision wrong, approach God for understanding. In Joshua 7:11-14, God revealed to Joshua the cause of his defeat by the people of Ai. Sometimes, in order to reveal your mistake to you, God may send you somebody to help you understand the situation.

2. We acknowledged our error

After gaining an understanding of the cause of the mistake, you will need to acknowledge and accept your error without blaming anyone else. You will need to take responsibility for your mistake.

> 2 Samuel 12:13: *"And David said unto Nathan, I have sinned against the LORD. And Nathan said unto David, The LORD also hath put away thy sin; thou shalt not die."*

In this verse, David admitted his sin when the prophet Nathan confronted him with it. This is a good attitude to take in all decisions – be honest. If you accept and take responsibility for your wrong decision, you will open up your spirit to receive divine revelation and guidance about the way forward.

3. We repented

After taking responsibility for the mistake, we repented of our errors. We became sober before God. A repentant heart will be clear before God about the mistakes made, and such a heart will be ready to do things differently in future. If you fail to show any sign of repentance, you are likely to commit the same mistake again. Repentance qualifies you for divine mercy that brings forgiveness.

> 1 John 1:9: *"If we confess our sins, he is faithful and just to forgive us our sins, and to cleanse us from all unrighteousness."*

Genuine repentance comes with confession to God and a readiness to change direction.

4. We forgave

To make a new start, we had to forgive ourselves for our own mistakes and forgive our friend for leading us astray. It wasn't intentional: our friend genuinely wanted to help us, even though it was against the way of God. So we forgave ourselves and forgave all those who offered us help that led to the failure. We did not entertain self-hatred or bitterness towards anybody.

> 2 Corinthians 2:10-11: *"To whom ye forgive any thing, I forgive also: for if I forgave any thing, to whom I forgave it, for your sakes forgave I it in the person of Christ; lest Satan should get an advantage of us: for we are not ignorant of his devices."*

If you fail to forgive those who were used by Satan to lure you into a wrong decision, you will fall into the trap and scheme of Satan.

5. We practiced restitution

Restitution means to right a wrong as much as is possible. If your decision caused loss to someone else, then you must do all you can to repay their loss. It is a practical demonstration of repentance. Restitution could entail returning all wrongly taken items to their rightful owner. It may also involve settling a debt or fulfilling a vow you have made.

In Genesis 20, Abimelech innocently took Sarah as his wife, but God told Abimelech to return Sarah to Abraham (verse 7) as she was Abraham's wife, and Abimelech obeyed (verse 14). He made his wrong right. This freed him from any form of accusation. When you make restitution, you close the door against your accuser.

6. We learned our lesson

When you seek the face of God regarding your wrong decision, you may learn many different things that will help you to make a better decision in the future. In my own family's example, we learned the following:

A. **When you fail to do the right things, you fail to stop the wrong thing from happening.** Whenever you notice anything going wrong in your decision, you should not ignore it. Amend the situation urgently, because it is a warning signal that there is a possibility of greater complications.

B. **Any error you allow to stay in your decision will influence your decision negatively.** If you do not attend to what is not right in your decision-making, you will soon lose control of the consequences.

C. **Operating in ignorance does not exonerate you from facing the reality of the situation.** There may be a good excuse for your ignorance but that will not be enough for you to escape its consequences. There were many things we did not know about our decision, but that did not protect us from its negative results.

D. **Anxiety and concerns about your future will open you up to Satan's deception.** When you become anxious about your tomorrow, it will give Satan the opportunity to sell you his ideas that will promise financial, economic, relationship or material securities, but they all end in losses.

E. **Not everything that appears good is godly.** Naturally, you will not embark on an idea unless it appears good, but unfortunately good appearances are not enough to guarantee success.

F. **A quick fix mentality is a journey to quick heart-brokenness.** Whatever or whoever promises you quick success should be approached with caution. Behind every great success is many days and nights of hard work. If you are being offered a fast, easy solution, be careful – there may be a catch or it may be a total deception.

G. **Whatever does not bring glory to the name of God, will not attract divine support.** If your decision glorifies man instead of God, it is not going to enjoy the support of heaven. God will not finance a project that will exalt man above His name. If your friend promises you assistance that seems to side-track the glory of your God, it is very unlikely to be of God.

H. **Satan is an intelligent creature with a brilliant knowledge of the Word of God.** Satan is able to quote Bible verses into your mind to deceive you into his plans, so be aware that not every thought that comes into your mind is of God, even if it's from the Bible. Not every Bible verse that springs to mind is evidence of the voice of the Spirit of God speaking to you. Satan can misuse Bible verses to deceive you. Individual Bible verses must be understood in context, not in isolation, and in relation to other Bible teaching on the same subject. You must check with God who is speaking into your mind: Satan or God, or your own memories, prompted by emotion. And check what else the Bible has to say on the same subject, so you get a balanced teaching.

I. **Quoting the Word of God is not enough, so appropriate it in the right way.** There are many verses in the Bible that could be applied to your situation, but that doesn't mean they should be. Each was originally given to address a specific situation and had a specific function – which may not always be appropriate for your situation, even if at first glance; it appears so. The wrong application of certain verses from the Bible can lead you down the wrong path.

J. **Not every helper is of God.** When people come to help you, ensure you check them out with God. Just as God can send you people to help you follow His direction, so Satan can send you people to help you unknowingly follow his plans.

K. **Emotion will rob you of the merits of insight.** When you are making decisions, get over your emotion. You will lose discernment and awareness of certain details if you don't. Emotion is a blind guide that leads you from darkness to darkness. Whatever gains control of your emotions will make you unaware of certain dangers. Therefore, avoid being emotional in your decision because you will lose touch with reality. Even good emotions, like the joy of anticipating the positive changes your decision will bring into your life, will hinder your sensitivity to hidden dangers and endanger your decision. The only exception is when we ask God for His peace about a certain decision, which we can receive to reassure us that we are making the right decision.

L. **If you talk to man before you talk to God about your decision, you will make the voice of man speak louder than God in your ears.** If you have already taken counsel from other people regarding your decision before you consult God, then when you do listen for God's voice, you may be hearing man's voice instead. If you don't want to fall into deception, put God first by speaking to Him first. Then stick to what God has told you, even if other people say the opposite.

M. **Sometimes, the line of demarcation between right and wrong, evil and good, can be very thin.** You must not rush into a decision because it looks good or right, but prayerfully investigate every detail, as there may be hidden details. What looks good may not always actually be good, so be thorough in your investigation.

N. **Not every process or procedure that goes smoothly is of God.** The fact that something goes without a hitch does not necessarily imply that it is of God. Do not judge the easiness of a process as always the sign of God's involvement. Satan can make a path smooth to lull you into his direction, just as much as he can make it rough to try to stop you going God's way. Discernment is always required.

RISK

Risk is an exposure to danger or a chance of loss or damage. Most decisions will involve a risk. This is because decisions involve a certain level of uncertainty. There are many unknowns involved in decision-taking. It is therefore important that you examine carefully the level of risk involved.

This is very pertinent when you have more than one option and your decision involves choosing between them. In such a situation, it is wise to pick the option with the lowest risk, unless you have a very good reason to expect a higher risk option to succeed.

In other situations, you may have only one option on the table, and it's a case of take it or leave it. However, there is still risk involved, because it may be riskier to stick with the status quo than to go with the one option on offer.

And then; there are certain decisions that clearly indicate high risk, yet it is right to go ahead for reasons of morality or faith.

> Esther 4:16: *"Go, gather together all the Jews that are present in Shushan, and fast ye for me, and neither eat nor drink three days, night or day: I also and my maidens will fast likewise; and so will I go in unto the king, which is not according to the law: and if I perish, I perish."*

In this story, Esther chose to appear before the king without an invitation from him. She prayed and fasted with her fellow Jews and then asked them to keep on interceding for her as she faced the risk. She was fully aware of the danger she was exposing herself to: *"If I perish, I perish."* At least, when you are aware of the risk your decision poses, it will help you to know how to prepare yourself.

Risks could be described as good or bad, depending on your motivation about it. A good risk is the one that involves stepping out in faith, believing that God will order your steps through the dangers on the way. It is a good risk when your decision is based on a clear divine instruction.

> Matthew 14:29: *"And he said, Come. And when Peter was come down out of the ship, he walked on the water, to go to Jesus."*

In this verse, Peter chose to walk on the water after receiving a word from Jesus Christ. He took a risk based on the trust he had on the spoken word of Jesus. Because his action was clearly based on obedience to Jesus, when he started sinking, Jesus stretched forth His hand to save him. Before you embark on a decision that will expose you to serious risk, ensure that you have the backing of God.

A bad risk, on the other hand, is when the decision is based on self-confidence, not God-confidence. If you face the unknown because you trust in your own strength and wisdom, it is a bad risk. This is because no matter how knowledgeable you may be, there will always be something you don't know about your decision. Therefore, if your confidence is in yourself rather than in God, your decision will be exposed to unknown factors, which will begin to manifest over time.

Proverbs 3:5 advises us to trust in the Lord with all our heart, without leaning on our own understanding. This is especially important in decisions involving faith, as Jesus said that we cannot bear fruit unless we are trusting in Him: "For without me; ye can do nothing" (John 15:5).

Similarly, a risk taken that tests or tempts God is a bad one. Stepping into the unknown to see whether God will act or not on your behalf is not advisable. In Exodus 17:2-7, Israel grumbled about their thirst and demanded that Moses give them water. Verse 2 and verse 7 describe this incident as an act of tempting God. If you make a demand to see if God will answer it or not, it is called tempting God. God will not support a decision taken to see whether He will act or not.

In Moses' case, God did supply the water, due to God's compassion for Moses and the people, not because they were testing Him. God will not perform miracles to prove doubters wrong – but he does respond to faith and out of compassion. Deuteronomy 6:16 commands us not to tempt God, or test him, as the NIV puts it: "Do not put the Lord your God to the test as you did at Massah." Jesus reinforced this teaching in Matthew 4:7.

Handling the Risk

1. Understand the risk

It is important that you have a detailed understanding of every risk attached to each of the options before you. Understanding the danger is far more important than the potential of the danger itself. With understanding, you will be able to explore how to manage the risk and navigate your way round it as you make your decision.

> Proverbs 4:7: *"Wisdom is the principal thing; therefore get wisdom: and with all thy getting get understanding."*

With understanding, you can brainstorm and analyse every bit of the risk you have identified in your decision. In Numbers 13:17-20, Moses sent some of the elders to spy the land they were about to invade. This was to give them a better understanding of the land before invasion. This exercise was intended to help Israel make the right decisions about how to conquer their enemies. Do your risk analysis to gain a better understanding of the situation, so that your response is effective.

2. Make a wise choice among the options

When you have more than one option as regards your decision, it is wise to take the option with the lowest risk, as we have said. Sometimes none of the options are low risk, but you can still work out what is the best of a bad bunch.

> 2 Kings 7:3-5: *"And there were four leprous men at the entering in of the gate: and they said one to another, Why sit we here until we die? If we say, We will enter into the city, then the famine is in the city, and we shall die there: and if we sit still here, we die also. Now therefore come, and let us fall unto the host of the Syrians: if they save us alive, we shall live; and if they kill us, we shall but die. And they rose up in the twilight, to go unto the camp of the Syrians: and when they were come to the uttermost part of the camp of Syria, behold, there was no man there."*

In this story, the four lepers faced three bad options. First, they could stay where they were, outside the city, and wait to either be killed by the Arameans when they arrived or die of hunger, whichever happened first. Their second option was to enter the city, where they might be safe for a while but would die of hunger eventually, because there was a famine in the city. Or finally, they could surrender to the Arameans in the hope of being spared and finding food in the Aramean camp, but at great risk of being slaughtered by them. At least their hunger would be over! Whichever option they chose had significant risk attached to it.

They chose to go to the camp of the enemy, and in so doing found that the Arameans had fled, leaving behind food and drink and treasures. The four lepers were saved. They were wise, because the first two options looked like certain death. At least the final option had a possibility of salvation, and in the end it saved their lives.

Unless you are doubly sure that God has told you to take one option among many alternatives, it is wise to pick the one with least risk.

3. Examine the work to be done

When you face many options, examine the level of work that needs to be done for each of the options. Where several options have the same outcome, it is wise to choose the option with least work, unless God has specifically told you that another option is right.

In Luke 14:28-32, Jesus advises us to count the cost attached to our actions – which can be in terms of the work involved, not just the price tag. Also, where you have many options, it can be wise to choose the one that is cheapest so that, if it goes wrong, you have suffered the least losses. But be careful of false economies, where the cheapest option can actually end up costing more because of low quality or reliability – and cost you more work to repair the damage or make replacements.

In any case, assess the level of work to be done to enable you to make a wise decision about whether the risk is really worth it.

4. Do self-examination

It is important for you to be real with yourself as you are making risky decisions. You will need to ask yourself if you have the attributes needed to meet the demands of your option.

In Exodus 13:17-18, God chose the longer route for Israel as they were coming out of Egypt, in order to avoid them facing battle early. God knew that if they went the short route, they might return to Egypt rather than fight the Philistines (verse 17). Going the longer route would avoid the Philistines and battles till the people were a long way from Egypt. God knew the Israelites better than they knew themselves! He knew their weaknesses.

So, we should examine our own strengths and weaknesses before making decisions, so that we ensure we have what it takes to carry out our decision. This will reduce the level of risk being taken.

5. Balance faith with reality

Faith is not realistic, but reality exists. Do not ignore the facts, even as you walk in faith. While the Bible encourages faith, it does not encourage self-deception.

> Proverbs 6:27-28: *"Can a man take fire in his bosom, and his clothes not be burned? Can one go upon hot coals, and his feet not be burned?"*

From these verses, it is clear that unless there is divine involvement, if you willingly enter into a fire, it will burn you. It is important to understand that there are certain experiences you will not be able to escape, irrespective of your level of faith. Therefore, as much as you act in faith, do not take unnecessary risks.

6. Listen inwardly

As you face risks, listen to the internal prompting of the Holy Spirit. In the midst of many alternatives, the Holy Spirit will be stirring up your spirit to guide you to the best option. Do not miss this inner prompting.

> Philippians 2:13: *"For it is God which worketh in you both to will and to do of his good pleasure."*

Through His Spirit that dwells inside you, God can and does speak to us, and we particularly need His wisdom when we cannot choose between risky options.

7. Progress with faith

Do not just start your decision-making with faith; you must also progress with faith. You need faith to determine a decision and you also need faith to implement the decision. Along the journey you will need faith.

For example, at the beginning of your decision, you may not have the necessary resources, but as you progress with faith, things begin to fall into place – if you keep trusting the Lord. Often He requires us to take steps of faith, and He gives us what is needed at each stage. Rarely are we given everything we need at the beginning, which keeps us trusting Him and staying close to Him as time goes on.

In Luke 9:3, Jesus sent out His disciples with nothing, but in Luke 22:35, they confessed that they lacked nothing. At the beginning of their trip, they had nothing but as they progressed in faith, the resources started falling into place for them. At the beginning, the risk was very high for them, but as they continued in faith, they overcame every risk. To deal with any risk, you will need the faith to believe that the God who started a good thing in your life will complete it, for His own glory.

8. Downsize your risk

No matter how big your risk is, your God is bigger. So do not overrate your risk. Make your decision based on the fact that your God is bigger than every risk both known and unknown.

> Numbers 13:33: *"And there we saw the giants, the sons of Anak, which come of the giants: and we were in our own sight as grasshoppers, and so we were in their sight."*

The Israelites who went into the land of Canaan to spy on the inhabitants came back with a bad report. They overrated their enemies and underrated themselves. They did not even consider their mighty God in their analysis. As they focussed on the strength of their enemies. They lost focus on the power of their God. Some risks make us afraid and it is that fear that makes us overestimate the problem – making the risk appear bigger to you than it really is. Don't let fear dictate your decisions and exaggerate the potential risks.

9. Set a limit for the level of the risk you will take

In your decision-making, avoid risks as much as possible. If your decision will involve a series of uncertainties, you will need to do a recheck. This is because many risks can lead to chaos and confusion.

In Luke 15:18, the prodigal son chose to return home after he decided that he couldn't bear his situation any longer. He had wasted his inheritance after prematurely asking his father for it, spending it all in a distant country. He decided the risk of returning home was less than the risk of staying where he was. He had reached the limit of the risk he was willing to endure in the land where he was living. In the same way, you need to know your limits, and set a ceiling for the level of risk you are willing to take in your decision-making – and don't go beyond it.

10. Create a safe environment for your risk handling

If you have identified the risk involved in your decision, ensure that you don't create a negative environment that will compound the risk. For example, if your decision will involve a group of individuals, ensure that you have a good relationship with them, otherwise, the disunity within your team will exacerbate the situation. Disunity is not a safe environment for risk-taking.

In John 13:34-35, Jesus taught his disciples to love each other. Love would create a safe environment for them as they faced an uncertain future, where persecution and hatred from enemies of the Gospel was waiting for them.

11. Develop a contingency plan for your risk

Do not face uncertainty without an escape plan. In case your decision does not turn out as envisaged, you will need to have a 'plan B' to avert any possible disaster. For example, it is not a wise decision to invest all your money into a business you have never been involved in before. If you do go ahead with an investment, only use some of your money and keep the rest to handle any eventuality.

1 Corinthians 10:13 states that God will always give us a way of escape from temptation, and similarly we should plan a way of escape when taking a risk, in case 'plan A' fails.

12. Practise effective communication with every person involved in the risk with you

If your decision will affect other people ensure that you communicate with them about the level of uncertainties involved in the decision. This will keep everybody at the same level of understanding about the situation. Uninformed team members may unintentionally make mistakes in decision implementation due to their lack of information.

In John 16:33, Jesus made it clear to His disciples that they would face persecution, but told them to be "be of good cheer; I have overcome the world." He communicated to them the potential dangers of the assignment He had given them. This created a common understanding among the disciples about the level of risk they faced.

13. Understand that risk management is not only about being smart but boldness

To face uncertainty will require boldness and courage. Be bold in the face of your uncertainty, because fear will make you stagger and lose composure and stability. This will put you in a very bad condition that may hinder your performance. In 1 Samuel 17:38, King Saul gave his armour to David to fight Goliath. Saul had the armour but he lacked the boldness to personally rise against Goliath. David had no armour but he had the courage to confront Goliath and so he won. Life is not only about being smart but being bold.

14. Decide to profit from your risk

Risk will expose you to a new experience that will benefit you in your future decision-making. So do not overlook the benefits of the risks you have encountered, applying your experience to your next exercise.

In 2 Kings 2, Elisha witnessed how Elijah divided the waters of the River Jordan on his way to being taken to heaven (verse 8). In verse 14, Elisha used the experience he had gained from that to divide the waters of the same river on his way back from chasing Elijah. The experience you gather today through the risks you take, will help you to face future challenges. Today's risk is preparing for a better tomorrow.

15. Know when to seek help

Sometimes, the risk you are taking will expose you to a situation that is beyond your expectations. You must be quick to seek help, otherwise, the situation may get worse and perhaps go beyond the point at which the damage can be repaired. In Matthew 14:28-31, when Peter saw that he was sinking, he shouted for help from Jesus. He took the risk to step into the water, but when he lost control of the situation, he did not keep silent. When you face unexpected challenges that threaten your decision, be quick to ask for help.

Nine

WISDOM FOR DECISION-MAKING

Wisdom can be described as the application of knowledge. The quality of your decision may be determined by the level of your wisdom. Your ability to perceive and walk in the guidance of God could also be determined by the level of your wisdom. In this chapter, we will explore areas you can study in order to gain wisdom to help you in your decision-making.

1. Fear of God

To fear God means to revere Him.

> Psalm 111:10: *"The fear of the LORD is the beginning of wisdom: a good understanding have all they that do his commandments: his praise endureth for ever."*

The fear of the Lord is to allow His Word to rule your life. When you live in obedience to His Word, His wisdom will dwell with you. When you make obedience to God's Word a habit, acting in wisdom becomes an automatic response in your situation.

In Genesis 41 and 42, Joseph allowed the fear of God to dictate his way of handling the situation, such that the ungodly pharaoh acknowledged the divine wisdom in Joseph. To gain access to the wisdom of God, you will need to live in total obedience to His Word.

2. Humility

To have humility is to have a low view and opinion of oneself.

> Proverbs 11:2: *"When pride cometh, then cometh shame: but with the lowly is wisdom."*

A man of lowly heart is open to receive wisdom because he is not blinded by his own ego and opinions. 1 Peter 5:5 states that God will always give grace to the humble. He will let wisdom dwell with the humble. If you want to operate in wisdom, choose to be humble.

A humble man does not despise himself but he does recognise his own weaknesses and the strengths of others. His heart is not filled with pride. He easily apologises for his mistakes. Humble people are not defensive when their choices or behaviour are questioned.

Humility allows divine guidance because a humble man is teachable, and this aids his good decision-making. When a humble man receives a favour, he considers it a gift not a right. A genuinely humble person prefers to serve other people instead of being served. The spirit of wisdom will always reside with a humble person. If you want to make your life a habitation of wisdom, make yourself humble.

3. Ask God for wisdom

> James 1:5: *"If any of you lack wisdom, let him ask of God, that giveth to all men liberally, and upbraideth not; and it shall be given him."*

Another way to gain wisdom for good decision-making is to intentionally ask God for wisdom. If you can make it your habit that before you make any decision you ask God for wisdom, then you will enjoy the flow of wisdom into your heart, which will birth good decisions.

If your decision involves choosing between many options, you can approach God for wisdom to discern which option is right, and you will enjoy divine guidance that will lead your heart into the right choice.

4. Search for wisdom

> Ecclesiastes 1:13: *"And I gave my heart to seek and search out by wisdom concerning all things that are done under heaven: this sore travail hath God given to the sons of man to be exercised therewith."*

It is possible to gain not only the gift of wisdom direct from God, but to understand wisdom better by finding it in the Bible. There are many relevant verses and stories that may address the kind of decision you want to make. As you study the Bible, ask the Spirit of the Lord to illuminate your mind and give you understanding. He will enable you to apply the Word of God to your situation.

There are also books written by credible people that will increase your wisdom if you read them. Similarly, in your attempt to search for wisdom, you can always ask the Holy Spirit questions that can birth wisdom. If you can spend time meditating on the issues of life and wait on the Lord for revelation, you will gain access into divine wisdom.

> Ecclesiastes 7:25: *"I applied mine heart to know, and to search, and to seek out wisdom, and the reason of things, and to know the wickedness of folly, even of foolishness and madness..."*

In your quiet time, you can ask the Spirit of God to reveal to you why certain things happen in your life and the reason for certain circumstances around you. The answers to these questions will increase your wisdom for decision-making. Learn how to probe and search for wisdom behind every event in your life, not just for the particular decision at hand.

5. Embrace wisdom

> Colossians 3:23: *"And whatsoever ye do, do it heartily, as to the Lord, and not unto men..."*

If you want to grow in wisdom for decision-making, you will need to be passionate and proactive about it. Set your heart on fire with a desire for wisdom – fall in love with wisdom! Without passion, heaven will not be moved to release wisdom to your heart. You need to convince heaven about your passion for wisdom. Your passion is an indication of how precious wisdom is to you. Heaven will not give you what you do not consider precious.

Your search for wisdom is part of your passion for God Himself, because true wisdom only comes from Him. Make your prayers for wisdom for decision-making passionate – not in an artificial way, like putting on an act – but through your genuine love for God and your desire to be more like Jesus.

6. Walk with the wise

> Proverbs 13:20: *"He that walketh with wise men shall be wise: but a companion of fools shall be destroyed."*

If you want to gain wisdom for decision-making, walk with the wise. In other words, find out who is wise and learn from them. Get to know them and befriend them if you can, because wisdom can be contagious. If you walk with the wise, you will tap into their wisdom. Wise people give wise counsel and guidance, sharing with you the wisdom that dwells in them.

7. Keep yourself under spiritual authority

> Deuteronomy 34:9: *"And Joshua the son of Nun was full of the spirit of wisdom; for Moses had laid his hands upon him: and the children of Israel hearkened unto him, and did as the LORD commanded Moses."*

Joshua served God under the authority of Moses, because Moses had laid his hands upon him. The 'laying on of hands' while praying for someone is a symbolic act of transference – the transfer of God's power to a person through us and our prayers. In this case, Moses's gift of wisdom had been transferred to Joshua.

If you genuinely serve the Lord under the spiritual authority of a Christian leader, God gives you the right to access the blessings

God has planted in that leader. Such blessings include the anointing of the Holy Spirit. If you want to flow in the wisdom of God, serve God in obedience under the authority God has planted over you. When your elders lay their hands on you, the virtues of the Spirit of God will flow into your life.

8. Seek counselling

To gain wisdom for decision-making, you may need to seek the counsel of wise people.

> Proverbs 11:14: *"Where no counsel is, the people fall: but in the multitude of counsellors there is safety."*

There are people who have done what you are about to do and they have their testimonies. If you seek counselling from such people, you will gain from their experiences and wisdom to forge ahead in your decision-making.

9. Learn from elders

> Job 12:12: *"With the ancient is wisdom; and in length of days understanding."*

When you have the privilege to be around elders who have diverse experiences, you can tap into their wisdom by observing their lifestyles. Monitor their ways of doing things and observe how they handle situations, and you will learn wisdom from them. Listen to their stories and what life has taught them. It is wise to learn lessons from those who have passed through certain challenges so that we do not fail in the same challenges. There is wisdom in elders.

> Job 32:7: *"I said, Days should speak, and multitude of years should teach wisdom."*

There is wisdom in experience. There are people around you who have passed through circumstances that you are about to face or are presently facing. You can learn a lot from their life encounters and apply it to your decision-making. Their failures and successes will be an asset to you for your decision-making.

10. Learn from life encounters

Ecclesiastes 1:16: *"I communed with mine own heart, saying, Lo, I am come to great estate, and have gotten more wisdom than all they that have been before me in Jerusalem: yea, my heart had great experience of wisdom and knowledge."*

Life is a teacher. In order to teach you wisdom, God sometimes allows you to face certain situations (both good and bad) that will enhance your wisdom for the future. In every situation of your life, ensure that you learn something valuable for your tomorrow.

BOOKS FROM THE SAME AUTHOUR

Journey to the Next Level

The New Creature

Building a Glorious Home:
A Pathway to a Successful Marriage

Words That Heal

The Enemy of Marriage

The Winning Formula

Faith that Always Wins:
Discover the Power of a Living Faith

Common Mistakes Parents make about their Children

Recovery is Possible

When You Are Desperate for a Miracle

This book and all other books from the same author are available at Christian bookstores and distributors worldwide.

They can also be obtained through online retail partners such as Amazon or by contacting the author at the address below:

Pastor Fatai Kasali
21-23 Stokescroft
Bristol
BS1 3PY
UK

Telephone: 00447727159581
E-mail: info@fkasali.com
Website: www.fkasali.com

www.ingramcontent.com/pod-product-compliance
Lightning Source LLC
Chambersburg PA
CBHW070507240426
43673CB00024B/467/J